"*Reading Raising Global Nomad.* ...... with a group of people who have arrived to guide you through life as an expatriate family. Pascoe is your big sister, your therapist, and your friend, telling you what to expect and how to handle the unexpected. You'll laugh, you'll cry, and by Monday morning you'll feel ready to roar. What a gift!"

~ ANNE COPELAND, DIRECTOR, INTERCHANGE INSTITUTE, BOSTON

"As her usual honest yet insightful self, Robin once again presents an incredibly realistic picture of the benefits and challenges of raising children internationally. Ultimately, this book provides hope to you, the reader. Robin shows you how to parent in a loving and affirming way."

~ MATTHEW NEIGH, SENIOR ASSOCIATE,
TRANSITION ASSOCIATES INTERNATIONAL

"This book is about change, what lies ahead, how to prepare for it, and how to deal with it. I particularly enjoyed the chapter about transforming global nomads into global citizens. After all, our children really want to make a difference in the world!"

~ SANDY THOMAS, DIRECTOR,
USA GIRL SCOUTS OVERSEAS, NEW YORK, N.Y.

"*Raising Global Nomads* is a road map for parents needing assurance that mobility is not a curse but an enriching experience for the entire family, including children. Robin has put my mind at rest about the global nomad choices I've made for my children."

~ YVONNE McNULTY, WWW.THETRAILINGSPOUSE.COM

"Thank you for your no-holds-barred, telling-it-like-it-is book on parenting global nomads. Having raised three of them myself, I know you have ticked all the boxes and hit on all the key issues we face living abroad."

~ YOLANDA HENRY, PAST PRESIDENT, AMERICAN WOMEN'S CLUB OF SURREY, U.K.

"Robin's most important book yet!"

~ JULIE SABIN, PARTNER, DOVETAIL RELOCATION, U.K.

Raising

Global Nomads

ALSO BY ROBIN PASCOE

A Moveable Marriage:
Relocate Your Relationship without Breaking It (2003)

Homeward Bound:
A Spouse's Guide to Repatriation (2000)

Culture Shock! A Parent's Guide (1993)

Culture Shock! A Wife's Guide (1992)

Raising
Global Nomads

PARENTING ABROAD IN AN ON-DEMAND WORLD

Robin Pascoe

EXPATRIATE PRESS

VANCOUVER

Expatriate Press Limited

1430 Terrace Avenue
North Vancouver, BC
Canada V7R 1B4
(604) 990-4532 (tel)
(604) 990-4598 (fax)
www.expatexpert.com

ISBN: 0-9686760-3-0

Edited by Barbara Pulling
Copyedited by Naomi Pauls
Cover and text design by Gabi Proctor/DesignGeist
Front cover photo by Inmagine
Back cover photo by iStockphoto
Author photo by Tamara Roberts

To Dave Pollock

With appreciation for your tireless work to reassure parents
of third culture kids. You inspired so many of us.

To my own parents, Herb and Bess Pascoe

With love and gratitude for teaching me well. I miss you both.

Contents

ACKNOWLEDGMENTS

I ONCE TOLD an audience in The Hague that I write my books out of gratitude for the wonderful and extraordinary life I have led as a wife, mother, writer, and traveler. My gratitude to all the inspirational women I have met around the world, truly knows no bound. So many people have made it possible for me to write this book and the others that came before it. It's time I started naming names, since throughout my books, spouses have always wanted to remain anonymous.

For their continued support, friendship, and hospitality on my many speaking trips, I'd like to thank in particular Jo Parfitt and Mary van der Boon.

For serving as my first "readers" on this book (and hosts and agents on so many occasions): Ann Lowey, Yolanda Henry, Ruth Buckmaster, Christine Lyon, Georgia Daugherty, and Julie Sabin of Dovetail Relocation in London.

For sponsoring my website and my travels: AMJ Campbell International and in particular Ole Jensen and Kevan Brown. Through their global network of fine moving companies, I have been able to bring my messages (and my books!) to countless destinations.

For always helping me with my research and serving as a sounding board: Yvonne McNulty, Anne Copeland, Barbara Schaetti, Lois Bushong, and Phyllis Adler.

For inspiration, Ruth Van Reken and the idea hatched at her kitchen table in Indianapolis that became the conference Families in Global Transition.

In Vancouver, I'm grateful to my close friend Cynthia McLean, who listened patiently while I tried to keep going; to my fine editors, Barbara Pulling and Naomi Pauls, and to my extremely talented book designer, Gabi Proctor.

Finally, I would have absolutely nothing to say were it not for Rodney, Lilly, and Jay. To say I'm grateful to them does not suffice. Simply put, I love them dearly.

INTRODUCTION

ONE EVENING SEVERAL years ago, I was invited to deliver a lecture at the American School in London, England. The school library was packed with parents of many nationalities. I found that gratifying, because I'm convinced it's important to write and speak about the universal challenges that expatriate families share. All parents need reassurance about raising their global nomads.

As a professional speaker, I remember that evening well for another reason. One mother in particular, sitting close to the front and privy to my sotto voce wisecracks about my husband, Rodney, chuckled throughout my presentation. I'm thrilled when I crack up a member of my audience, since humour can break through the reluctance many people have to openly discussing the serious yet common issues of expatriate life.

Afterwards, when all of the questions from parents had been answered, I sat down at a table to sign copies of my books. When a teenage girl approached me, I was surprised at first. I don't encourage students to attend my parent talks, or vice versa. I like everyone to feel free to offer comments when I speak, and having both sides of the family present can inhibit that kind of interaction.

But this young girl was terribly earnest.

"How do you *know* all of this?" she asked. "You not only nailed my mother's life perfectly, but you just described mine, too. Did you move around a lot when you were a kid?"

I replied that I hadn't. Then, because I was exhausted and overcaffeinated, I slipped into my default response position. "I'm a journalist," I said. "That means I interview many people and do a lot of research for my work."

She went away still certain I must be a mind reader or personally acquainted with her parents. For my part, I didn't think about the encounter again until six months later. I was back in the U.K. to lecture at another international school, the Hillingdon campus of ACS International Schools. The entire high school population, more than two hundred students, were there to learn about their identities and challenges as global nomads. It was springtime, and as in most international schools, a significant turnover in the school population was just around the corner. Truth be told, as I listened to the students noisily take their seats in the auditorium, I felt more terrified of speaking to these teenagers than of facing their parents that evening.

I began by taking the easy road, shamelessly using my son, Jay, as a way into their heads and hearts. Jay was a high school senior at the time, and so I could flawlessly imitate the fashionable teenspeak of the day. I said *yo* a lot and made every sentence short and clipped. I also shared with my audience the fact that I had sought my son's advice on how to successfully address a high school assembly.

"I wouldn't know, Mom," he told me. "I skip assemblies." Naturally, his response got a huge laugh from the crowd. Then, for some inexplicable reason, I made a snap decision to veer off script: I told them about my exchange with the young American School in London student six months earlier. The two schools are rivals in sports, as it turns out, so the mere mention of that other school whipped up the crowd. I thought for sure I would lose them at that point, but they quieted down. My heart started to race, because the answer I should have provided to that ASL student at the time had suddenly come to me. It was an unexpected and exciting moment.

"Actually, I never moved around when I was a kid like all of you have done," I began tentatively. "In fact, I lived in the same house on the same street in Toronto until I was sixteen." The students appeared to be listening. My brain was zooming ahead, piecing together my personal history and experience.

"But when I was twelve, my life was turned upside down. My mother died very suddenly and life changed overnight for my family." I paused there for a minute, gauging their reaction. The room was still. Being kids, I knew they probably were wondering how she died. Not wanting to go into the details of a brain aneurysm, I said, "Basically, something in her head exploded and the doctors couldn't fix it." That certainly got their attention.

"When I was sixteen, my father remarried. We moved out of the only house I had ever known. Not to another city, like London, although it might as well have been, since it was far from the neighbourhood where I had grown up. Even though I was entering my final year of high school, my dad decided that I would be better off in a private girls' school, as a day student. So I got yanked away from my lifelong friends and, worse, had to go to this snobby school—with a uniform!—that didn't even have the one thing I was really interested in, which was a band and an orchestra. My entire high school life had been about playing the flute and the piccolo."

I distracted the students with some jokes about how awful I looked in the dreadful green tunic with gold blouse and green tie, knee socks and blazer, all set off with black oxford shoes. I think trying to picture me in that getup (think Barbra Streisand at the age of sixteen in a private school uniform) provided some comic relief from the traumatic part of my story. After all, this was a bit like Bambi's mother dying before the movie even got going.

I knew there were some students listening who would be repatriating with their families to the U.S. for their final year of high school. I didn't want anyone freaking out before I even started my prepared talk. So I fudged things a bit by saying "Of course, I made *tons* of new friends at the private school." This was not quite a lie; I do recall making at least one friend about halfway through the year. I didn't share the truth with my audience, which was that that year would have been the worst year of my life if I hadn't already experienced that when I was twelve. Despite almost failing that school year, arguing more with my newlywed father than I ever had before, resenting the marriage that had created this awful scenario for me, and missing my own mother desperately as only a teenage girl can do, I did survive that last year of high school. More amazingly, I managed to get into college.

If I had been able to answer that young girl at the American School in London honestly, I would have told her that, while not mobile as a kid, I indeed knew what it was like to go through a profound change as a young person. I would also like to thank her now for helping me see how my personal and professional lives have managed to merge, and so happily, too.

Given the traumatic loss I experienced near the beginning of my life, how *did* things manage to turn out so well? The answer to that question arrived accidentally, as many insights do, on that innocuous day when I was worried about falling flat on my face in front of an auditorium full of teenagers. I was all of a sudden crystal clear about why my own life had turned out the way it had: I had had the unconditional love and support of my family.

Not a terribly earth-shattering revelation, to be sure, but so relevant for families on the move. And I realized it was the major theme that has informed my work with expatriates and their families for more than twenty years. Give families the support they need to make them feel safe and worthy, I tell businesses who send employees abroad, and they will thrive just as children who are supported thrive. I have always known that I am loved and have always felt protected by my family (including Rodney and our two children), even though circumstances have forced me make a lot of decisions on my own.

"When I speak to your parents tonight, that's basically what I'm going to tell them," I said to that roomful of teenagers. "Make sure your children know you love them; make them feel safe; protect them without overprotecting them, so they can learn to stand on their own two feet. I want to be sure they know that, despite all the moving around, they, as loving parents, are your true home and bedrock of support. At the end of the day, that's the parent's prime directive."

And then, placing my own magic moment of insight aside, I couldn't resist throwing out one last cliché. "There is an old saying: what doesn't kill you makes you stronger." I heard a few groans from the audience, which I found reassuring. They were, after all, teenagers.

A lot has changed since the early 1990s when I wrote my first book for expat parents, *Culture Shock! A Parent's Guide.* At that time, an airless, windowless mahjong room at the Lido Club in Beijing served as my office, because our living quarters did not provide me with a workroom of my own. From there, we moved back to Ottawa and then on to Seoul, finally ending up in Vancouver, British Columbia. As the "Expat Expert" (also the name of the website I began publishing in late 1998, which attracts visitors from over a hundred countries), I have traveled to speak all over the world, from Johannesburg to Shanghai to Jerusalem: to women's clubs, to international schools, and to business audiences. Since those early days, too, the world has become globalized, digitalized, and, sadly, terrorized. That's the big picture that will be examined in these pages.

On the home front, my day job for well over twenty years, raising our two children, has ended. Lilly, who was born in Bangkok in 1983 and who made six international moves before she was thirteen, has finished university and started her career as an international environmental activist. Jamie, who has now assumed the more adult handle of Jay, was born in Ottawa in 1987 and made five moves before he was nine. After a year off following high school, he is now at university. Of course, I'll be parenting forever, but my kids already need me in different ways. Naturally, I'm dealing with empty-nest syndrome and the inevitable withdrawal pains from nurturing. I feel alternately depressed and elated. My really hard work is done, and I'm feeling a lot of sadness. But I am able to look back now, to see what worked and what didn't, and to share with readers the lessons I learned.

There is also a sense of relief that we all survived the growing years to reap the numerous positive legacies of a global life. Lilly and Jay's view of the world, their values, the friends they made, and their feeling that they are somehow different have been influenced by the international mobility precipitated by their father's first career as a diplomat. Even after our repatriation to Canada, their very beings continued to scream *global* as Rodney began a second career, traveling all over the world marketing Canadian education.

"Where's Dad today?" my son has asked over the years when Rodney didn't show up for supper.

"Dubai," I would reply. Or São Paulo, or Istanbul, or somewhere equally "out there."

Lilly and Jay are products of their early childhood experiences and their constant exposure as teenagers to the global workplace of their parents. They have also been lucky enough to continue jumping on planes to faraway places, thanks to school field trips and their father's considerable accumulation of air miles.

"My father may be a retired foreign service officer," an adult third culture kid once told me, "but I can never be a retired foreign service kid."

Growing up motherless might have contributed to my personal decision to choose my children over a career, but I'm keenly aware that I had the economic luxury to make that choice. Even after repatriating to Canada, when a second income would have been helpful, I stuck with my choice because, like most global managers, Rodney was forced to step up his road-warrior activities. This required that he spend a great amount of time away from our home—and away from the children during important years. Someone had to keep an eye on the home front. I continued to pursue my writing life, but I always placed Lilly and Jay's needs first.

I believe this was a good choice—for *my* family. As in all matters of culture, there is no one right way to parent well, only different ways. Global nomads are raised for the most part by parents living far from home and family; these parents must rely on their natural instincts, the support of new communities, and whatever resources they can find to help them make their decisions.

Every family is unique and will require different choices. Moreover, we all make mistakes. It's worth remembering, as most of us teach our children, that human beings learn from failure as well as from success. There are lessons to be learned from even our less-than-finest moments and from the experiences, both good and bad, of others.

I feel confident in delivering some good news at the outset: *Most children turn out great!* I'm always at pains to pass on this extremely positive message to expat parents. However, I immediately qualify my comment by adding that proactive parenting abroad is a necessity; children need their parents *more* after they have been uprooted, not less. Too many couples disappear into the hectic expat social scene or workplace soon after arrival in a new place, leaving young children with a local caregiver who may eventually become a treasured member of the family but in the early days is just a scary stranger.

By proactive parenting, I don't mean overparenting, though. Even in the insular and sheltered expatriate world, children need to learn how to lead their own lives, independent from their parents. Otherwise, they will be ill prepared to be launched into the adult world that awaits them and become global citizens.

Only recently have children's transition challenges and cross-cultural adjustments begun to be highlighted by an industry of intercultural trainers, coaches, and researchers; by organizations sending families abroad, and by the international schools expat children attend. It was tempting in the past for some parents to gloss over their children's mobility challenges (and their own, too), in an attempt to get everything and everyone moving smoothly. Kids were told to just get on with it. Now there are numerous excellent books, articles, and websites that shed light on the third culture kid experience and on what adult TCKs have shown they are capable of contributing to the new globalized world. I will be quoting from some of these sources, and I list many more in the resources section at the back of this book.

Raising Global Nomads, however, is different from these resources. It identifies many of the complexities of growing up as a global nomad so that parents can give their children the skills and knowledge they need. It focuses not only on the critical role parents play in their children's transitions but on the impact different parenting styles can have on the choices children make later in their lives. I conclude the book by celebrating the notion that global nomads, as declared by sociologist Ted Ward back in 1984, are the "prototype citizens" of the future. Indeed, the terms "global nomad" and "global citizen" go together nicely. But nothing happens by accident. Like parents everywhere, expat parents need to guide their children into happy, productive, and independent lives wherever they may choose to live in the world.

Parents posted abroad, away from their own family support systems, may be unaware of how their own behaviour and actions transfer onto their children. And too often, the important part that parents play gets lost in the intense dissection of third culture kids by academics, educators, and psychologists. Parents want to know *how* to deal with a toddler or teenager who is acting up, not only *why* it's happening. For that reason, this book also explores the ways in which adult issues associated with expatriate life (the moveable marriage, work-life balance challenges, culture shock, the cellular ties that bind) affect child-rearing being done far from home.

Obviously I can't cover everything there is to know about parenting abroad in a few hundred pages. What I *can* do is get you started on thinking about some of the challenges, so that you can forge your own parenting strategies in a positive, optimistic context.

To help me do this, I have enlisted the aid of two of my colleagues in the Families in Global Transition movement. Readers are fortunate to be able to read the insights into third culture kid identity development presented by Barbara Schaetti, who is well known and well respected in the intercultural field. The daughter of an oil executive, Schaetti made multiple moves in her childhood.

Chapter 8 also features advice from marriage and family therapist Lois Bushong, who examines the mental health challenges of global nomads and their families. Bushong spent her childhood in Central America as the child of missionaries. As an adult, she has chosen to work with the missionary community, to whom expatriate parents worldwide owe a huge debt of gratitude. Much of the research on global nomads and third culture kids grew out of the missionary experience, not the corporate, diplomatic, or military worlds.

Finally, I hope readers will learn from, and chuckle over, my own parenting gaffes in all their foolish glory. Nothing would make me happier than a reader who puts down the book and says: "*I* could have written this!" I'm hoping my stories are *your* stories, with different places and dates and children plugged in.

Nobody is perfect. I know I did get some things right, though. Despite being moved around a lot as kids, Lilly and Jay have their feet firmly planted on the ground, wherever they happen to find themselves. They know that change can be a good thing, and they certainly know they are loved. Independent, self-sufficient, kind, and respectful of others: I can ask nothing more of them as they begin their adult lives. They are two of the three great success stories of my life.

The third? That would have to be my long and happy marriage to their terrific father. After all, I can't take all the credit.

Chapter 1

UNDERSTANDING YOUR GLOBAL NOMAD

THE FOUR OF US sat around our dinner table in Vancouver as Lilly contemplated career choices and university applications. In her final year of high school, she had decided she wanted to work internationally on environmental issues. Rodney and I figured this was a no-brainer. Always a focused student, Lilly was only eight years old when she announced her commitment to saving the planet to the members of her Beijing Brownie troop.

Rodney was working at the Canadian embassy in Beijing at that time. I had volunteered to help supervise a Brownie troop at her international school, but Lilly wanted to start an environmental club. I thought I was being terribly clever by suggesting they become the environmental Brownies. Daily life in China was still pretty basic then, and Beijing qualified as a hardship posting. Most of the toilets, for example, both at our apartment in a run-down diplomatic compound and at the school, ran water long after someone had finished using them. If nothing else, I figured a gaggle of young girls dashing around the school, clicking toilet handles to make the water stop running, would be a useful and environmentally friendly activity. There certainly weren't any nature trails just outside the school door.

Back at our dinner table in Canada, her father piped in with the opinion that Lilly might consider joining the foreign service if she were keen to live and work globally. Before Rodney could even finish his sentence (or I could remind him that he had left the government out of bureaucratic frustration), Jay jumped all over his sister, indirectly taking aim at his father. "Don't you *ever* do that to your kids!" he said with more emotion than any of us had ever witnessed from him, except over the score of a hockey game.

Where on earth had *that* come from?

Still addressing his sister, Jay elaborated, and quite fiercely, too, "Don't start dragging your kids around the world every few years, making them feel like outsiders in a new school and making them get used to foreign places where people want to pinch you all the time. I would *never* do that to my kids!"

An expat version of Murphy's Law holds that if you move around with two children in tow, one will grow up wanting to go global and the other will want to stay put and hug a tree. Despite all evidence to the contrary, we had just met the real tree hugger in the family.

THE LEGACY OF MOVING

The months following that dinner-table outburst were leading up to Jay's transfer to a large, impersonal high school from the cozy elementary school nearby. He had been at the elementary school for almost four years, ever since we had moved to Vancouver, and after a rocky start, he was comfortable with the school and the friends he had made. But now I sensed something was not quite right. Jay's mood was not as even-keeled as it had been, and the changes in his behaviour baffled me. He would be moving up to high school with a cohort he knew well. So, what was the problem? Twitchy and nervous on the subject, he definitely didn't want to talk about it.

I raised my concerns with his father.

"Hey, Expat Expert," said Rodney, "did you ever consider that your son is nervous because change is in the wind? His sister is moving on to university, and he's graduating from elementary school. Or that maybe the idea of changing schools is dredging up unpleasant memories of being dragged to so many different postings in his younger years?"

Rodney reminded me of something I travel around the world lecturing about: the fact that, even once they stop moving, children retain the legacy of a nomadic childhood. One mother I would later meet, an Australian expat spouse whose family has lived in both Asia and Europe, puts it this way: "I've heard so many people talk about their plans to get the children back to their home country by a certain age, as if there is a window of time during which you can go back through the wardrobe, à la Narnia, and it will be like you'd never left. But we are all changed by the experience, from the very first conversation we have with the children about an impending move."

In my own home, I had managed to miss all the signs of the lifelong impact of global mobility. I was reminded yet again of how our children keep us humble. I soon found a quiet moment to discuss his upcoming move to high school gently with my son, emphasizing that change doesn't always mean unsettledness but can be something positive. I reminded him of all the moves he had made that had turned out happily. There was no reason to believe, I pointed out, that his entry into high school would be anything less than a resounding success.

After that day, it was smooth sailing—except for the fact that Jay fretted about being short. He was on his own, I told him, with that one.

WHO IS A GLOBAL NOMAD?

The label "global nomad" is used interchangeably with the term "third culture kid." Norma McCaig, who has tirelessly brought the needs of mobile kids to the forefront, defines a global nomad as "anyone who has ever lived abroad before adulthood because of a parent's occupational choice."

Ruth Van Reken and the late Dave Pollock, the gurus on TCKs, define one in their book *Third Culture Kids* as "a person who has spent a significant part of his or her developmental years outside of the parents' culture." I will refer often in this book to Pollock and Van Reken's ground-breaking work, but I like McCaig's definition since it includes the parent's occupation. In the expat world, the reality is that the majority of working partners are fathers, even if more women are accepting overseas assignments. And it is the father's occupation—often a job that places heavy demands on his time and energy—that directly impacts the nurturing of global nomads, especially in today's world of skewed work-family balance. The expat father, quite simply, is often not around, and that has a profound effect on the family dynamics.

THE PROFILE OF A GLOBAL NOMAD

Most publications about global nomads and third culture kids, including my previous books, are quick to paint a profile of the child who grows up overseas. Many of the character traits identified in these profiles are generalizations, and I've had some of them challenged by outspoken and articulate teenage expats. But these top six character traits are nonetheless a useful starting point, and one that should provide reassurance for many parents. A point to keep in mind as you read through them is that these traits don't necessarily describe your children as they are *now* but are glimpses into who they may become.

1. Alert, intelligent, and geographically aware

Global nomads inhabit a wider world than most kids; a newspaper headline may make sense to them because they have lived in the country in question, visited the place, or have a friend from there.

"When a global nomad reads the news, they can often picture what's happening thousands of miles away," writes grown-up global nomad Debra Carlson on WorldWeave.com. "This does not generally apply to kids who grow up in one culture… A global nomad feels connected to events taking place all over the world. We recognize that people everywhere share the joys and pains of life. We've lived, felt, smelled, heard and witnessed wide swaths of human experience."

More than a few global nomads who watched the horror of the 2004 Asian tsunami unfold in the media, for instance, no doubt remembered lying on that beach in Thailand or visiting neighbouring Southeast Asian nations on holiday. I know as a parent, the pain in the face of a small blond-haired boy roaming around looking for his mother forced me to turn off my television.

In a world in which global diversity must be respected more than at any other time in history, global nomads take diversity in their everyday stride.

2. Mature, sensitive and skilled at listening

That global nomads may possess a greater ability to listen brought guffaws from one teenage audience I spoke to (although they must be good listeners to have those mobile phones glued to their ears all day). But as I've often pointed out to parents, global nomads spend a lot more time with adults during their childhood than do their stationary counterparts. They learn how to introduce and present themselves because they are called upon to do so more often.

I love to share the story of my daughter's toddler play group in Bangkok to illustrate this accelerated maturity. About a dozen eighteen-month-olds would stand around our apartment with a cup of apple juice in one hand and a small bowl of fruit and cheese in the other while they "chatted" amicably with their little friends. The scene was so like a cocktail party with miniature guests that I wouldn't have been shocked if, one day, one of the toddlers had pulled a business card out of a diaper.

Constant exposure to adults—so much entertaining goes on in expat life—lends an air of maturity to these youngsters, even if they may gag when no one is looking over being forced to meet yet another crowd of strangers around their parents' dining-room table. In the non-mobile world, young people mingle much less often with adults, taking all their cues from their peer group. This is limiting, especially when they later enter a workforce that contains people of a variety of ages. Exposure to adults who are not teachers or celebrity icons, even if the expatriate world is mostly made up of middle-class professionals, is a bonus for global nomads. Their personal history of successful transition experiences, extensive travel, and international school field trips can also make global nomads feel worldly-wise and older than their years.

3. Likely to exhibit tolerance and cross-cultural understanding

Living in Vancouver, one of the most multicultural cities in the world, our children attended schools that reflected Canada's diversity. But although multicultural, these schools were not intercultural, as are international schools where kids of different nationalities mix instead of staying in separate bubbles. As an expat parent, when you check out your child's class picture or school team, you see a mini United Nations.

By studying in culturally diverse classrooms, global nomads learn from an early age that there is more than one way to see the world. "We don't assume that our way is the best or only way," writer Debra Carlson observes. "We are life-long learners, and the world is our classroom. These are critical skills in a world looking for economic prosperity and peace, when in the past there has been a tendency to destroy what we don't understand and annihilate those who are different."

Cross-cultural understanding and empathy are, I repeat, bonuses going into the world of today.

4. Flexible and open to change

Flexibility becomes ingrained in a mobile child; without it, he or she is doomed to misery. Change is the buzzword for these kids, as they feel it constantly. Change is a fact of expat life. However, flexible children don't necessarily start out that way, as one mother based in Europe shared with me about her preteen daughter: "She always likes to know what to expect and doesn't like to be taken by surprise with changes to plans. She's not at all hardwired to be a corporate global nomad, especially with my husband's multinational company, which is renowned for moving employees frequently and unexpectedly. However, now living in her third country away from home, I can see that she is far more comfortable with change and flexible in all sorts of things. It has forced her to learn a different attitude towards change, one that didn't come naturally to her. If I had looked at any list of characteristics of a global nomad before our first move I would have said she would probably not be a good candidate for it, and yet she has become one, and is really thriving."

5. High achieving

There is always laughter when this point is thrown out to teenagers, but it's true. Many children, my own included, attended international schools where a premium was placed on performance in the classroom over that on the football field. (Of course, being good at sports has never hurt a child's chance at popularity.) Children abroad work hard at their studies in order to fit into what's considered normal, although the same behaviour may relegate a child to the geeky group at home. Likewise, as noted earlier, the adults to whom children are exposed in expatriate communities are usually skilled professionals with a record of high achievement.

6. Drawn to careers associated with service to the community or the world

My daughter's career choice in international development and environmental studies is not unusual in the least. Since she keeps in regular touch with some of the global nomads she grew up with, we've learned that these young adults favour the kind of work that will take them abroad. In combination with the traits listed above, their professional preferences make them highly valuable to recruiters for companies that now operate globally.

Global nomads have most likely seen poverty and despair up close. They feel grateful for their own good fortune and want to help others improve the quality of their lives.

CHALLENGES FOR GLOBAL NOMADS

As we've seen, there are advantages for global nomads in having spent their formative years abroad. However, there are challenges unique to these children that parents must be vigilant to keep in balance. Allow me to highlight some of these.

• *The overseas experience makes them feel different.*

Global nomads feel different when placed among children who have never moved or traveled extensively. There exists a huge experience gap between these two groups. While your child can picture what life looks like at "home" (well, sort of), someone who has never left home sees life abroad only through the inflated, often hyper images flashed on satellite television. Expat kids may feel snobbish because of their experiences. (It can't hurt to keep reminding them that they have been privileged to travel.) And although it may sound pretentious to their peers, the fact is they *have* traveled or lived in exotic places. In a desire to fit in upon repatriation, a global nomad may not tell peers where he has lived unless "outed" by a new teacher. Some children aren't believed, either, when they tell their teachers or peers that they have been to so many places, so they keep quiet to avoid being labeled liars.

Global nomads also get the idea that they are special. When they come home on leave with their families, much fuss and too many gifts are dispensed, as if Christmas has come in July. Some children may also be used to being stared at overseas if they have blond hair or white skin. Although they may protest about these "stare squads," many children, especially young ones, admit to missing the attention when they return to an environment where they don't stand out.

For all these reasons, parents of global nomads need to avoid giving their children a heightened sense of self-worth and entitlement, which too often translates into arrogance. Parents who feel guilty about moving their children may overcompensate with material goods or heap on the praise at times when constructive criticism might be more helpful.

"I'm working so hard to balance that notion of being special with 'normal' and 'average,'" one spouse wrote to me. "I've tried helping my children keep their expat lifestyle in perspective by pointing out to them that they're not special so much as privileged. We try to balance their lives with 'normal' activities for them, such as chores at home during the school year or working at jobs that require hard, physical labour on a consistent daily basis in the summer. If nothing else, they understand the future value of going to college right now."

Teaching your children about their responsibilities as well as their rights is important for parents everywhere. That duty becomes absolutely critical if your children are bred in the affluent mirage that is the expatriate lifestyle in many parts of the world. But remember, even children living so-called privileged lives are allowed to have challenges.

• *They gravitate to others like themselves.*
Global nomads find it difficult to articulate the impact of everything they have absorbed unless they are with children who grew up as they did. I like to use the airport waiting lounge as an example. Expat families waiting for glamorous charters to Borneo or a South African safari recognize each other by the experience they wear as a family, and they can immediately launch into "automatic pilot" conversations that last up to twenty minutes without even thinking what to say next.

"So, what's your international school like?"

"What's the shopping like where you are, and what have you bought?"

"Have you been to _____?"

When you are living overseas in a milieu of similar families, your children will have no trouble finding friends to whom they can relate. The challenges will come later, when you repatriate to communities where no one has ever moved around or when youngsters become college bound.

- *Children are silent partners in relocation.*

This is another point always to keep in mind: your children don't move by choice. An adult does have a choice (although most spouses know the choice is often between yes and yes, and that's not a typo). You can offer your children a say in some matters and solicit their feedback, and of course they can also help with the packing up. But at the end of the day, they are going, whether they like it or not, along with the lamps and the coffee table.

"I don't trade on the flexibility factor," one mother told me. "So many people have said to me, after asking how the children feel about moving, that of course children are so flexible, they'll be fine. It can be true, but I don't use that as an excuse to ignore their many and varied needs throughout the ordeal of moving. Just because they are flexible doesn't mean that the move isn't challenging for them."

But, this mother added, "I also try to remember that while they are resenting the fact they have no say in it, they don't yet know the riches that may be in store for them as a result of the experiences they are having. Neither do we as the parents, but I have seen and heard enough to know that there are potentially some real benefits to growing up this way."

Lack of control over your move may be a source of frustration or feelings of powerlessness for your kids, and of guilt for you. Children can easily play on a parent's emotions and manipulate them to get their own way. Once in a while, that's not a problem. But permissive parenting—forgoing limits because you are wracked with guilt—can come back to haunt you when the children are older and still have no notion of boundaries.

• *Issues of adolescence and rebellion are delayed.*
It's hard to grow up rebellious in a country far from home where getting away from the family may not be an option. So many global nomads store up their rebellion for later. I've warned parents who are sending their children off to university, for instance, to expect a magnification of the free-for-all first year away. Many teenagers will act up when they leave home for the first time. Dorm rooms were designed for this purpose. But a child who has been reined in over the years, even if she wears that veneer of maturity, is still a young person who needs to test her limits. Global nomads do this later than most.

There are also life skills that are delayed by living overseas. Lack of a driver's license is the skill most commonly lamented by young global nomads returning "home" for college.

Part-time jobs, not to mention the financial experience and independence these bring, have always been problematic for expat teens because of work permits. I understand this issue well from being a spouse, but work experience does not have to be just about a paycheck. It's about taking responsibility, showing up on time, and toughing it out when you feel like quitting. Volunteer positions can fill these requirements, as can babysitting, tutoring, mentoring, or any other creative ideas that may have to be suggested by parents.

Don't give your kids blanket dispensation from doing work around the home, either. When we lived in Seoul and had the good fortune to have live-in help, I still made sure to do many of the daily chores myself. It's the oldest parental tool in the kit—role modeling—and it applies to everything from a work ethic to a social conscience.

Spoiled as we were to have someone make us dinner every night, my children were still expected to set and clear the table as well as to make their own beds and keep their rooms tidy. This ability to understand that we as a family were responsible for the upkeep of our home came in handy when we repatriated to Canada and my children and husband reluctantly became members of the "clean team." Every weekend, we cleaned our house from top to bottom. My daughter became so good at cleaning toilets that one of her first summer jobs was as a chambermaid at a bed-and-breakfast.

• *A migratory instinct can take hold.*
Like birds who feel the shift in weather, a young person uprooted every two years or so may feel the urge to keep moving on. This has consequences later in life for some, who feel they cannot settle down. "Somehow the settling down never quite happens. The present is never enough—something always seems lacking. An unrealistic attachment to the past, or persistent expectation that the next place will finally be home, can lead to this inner restlessness that keeps the TCK always moving," write the authors of *Third Culture Kids*.

For some global nomads, this restlessness can also spill over into difficulties in maintaining relationships. An American spouse told me: "The first time I ever heard the term 'global nomad' was at a lecture I attended six months into our first overseas assignment in Indonesia. What stayed with me most was how global nomads have a harder time with long-term relationships than people who live in the same community all their lives."

Her workshop leader offered some great advice for

parents, which is worth repeating here: teach your children to keep in contact with friends who have moved on, and encourage contact with family and friends they have left behind. Make sure they have an opportunity to see these people as often as possible, too, including friends from the expatriate community who may be in your vicinity during their home leave. "I've kept his advice in the back of my mind for the last ten years," this mother said. "I want my sons to know how to maintain relationships over the long haul. I feel it's of utmost importance to them for their future happiness in marriage and family."

- *Global nomads feel rootless and restless, as if they don't belong anywhere.*

The two questions most likely to tongue-tie a global nomad are "Where are you from?" and "Where is home?" Both of these are tantamount to asking "Who are you?"

I like to compare the "Where are you from?" question asked of a mobile child with the question "And what do you do?" often asked of the mother. Both can elicit the same befuddled and angst-ridden response, and there is no direct, easy answer unless the listener has a few hours to spare. Everyone struggles with identity challenges at some point or another. Mobile children are forced to confront these more often.

As I wrote in my book *A Parent's Guide,* the two questions can have several meanings at once. "Do you mean where was I born," the TCK may ask, "or where am I living now?" "Where are my parents living?" is another possibility. The answer to "Where are my clothes at this precise moment?" may offer yet another road to the answer.

Marriage and family therapist Lois Bushong points

out that siblings may also respond differently to the same question. From her personal family experience, she remembers when the question "Where are you from?" was asked and she would reply, "We live in Honduras." Her brother, though, would say, "We are from Ohio."

The way children respond to the "Where is home?" question may be connected to their relationship with their parents, too. What's home for Mom and Dad is not always home for the children. The issue often arises in discussions when a family is about to embark on home leave. Their mother may be going on and on about what they will do when they get "home," but children can't muster the same enthusiasm; to them, it's not home at all.

Sometimes even the home the family is currently living in can be a source of friction between the global nomad and her parent. As a straight-shooting young girl who spoke to me put it, and quite belligerently, "Why does my mother feel that every house we live in should be a home? It's not a home. It's a house!"

Home for global nomads is an emotional place, not a geographical location. In simple terms, home is where they don't need to explain themselves. I've always told people that, after moving around for most of my adult life, I feel at home at a family event like a Bar Mitzvah or a wedding. With family, I don't have to hand out a program.

When my own children were old enough, I gave them some talking points they could use to shut down unsettling conversations about where they were from or where home was. Among other advice, I suggested the following strategy: "Tell them 'My nationality is Canadian. Right now, my father's job has taken us to _____.' " Having an answer at the ready made them feel better. Of course, we had to make a slight adjustment when we moved home to Canada and my daughter's new friends reacted to her response with "Duh!"

Every family comes up with its own strategy for staying connected. "I like people to visit us," an Australian mother told me, "so that when we maintain contact by phone or e-mail, when we visit them, or move home and try to pick up our life there, we don't have to explain ourselves, at least not as much. People at home then at least have some understanding of our experiences, our lifestyle, our friends in that other life."

Summer holidays also provide a great opportunity to give your children a sense of connection to their home culture. During July, we placed both of our children in summer camps in Canada, and we sometimes rented a cottage not far from our permanent residence at the time.

• *Global nomads have issues of unresolved grief.*
One of the biggest challenges associated with growing up global is accumulating so many losses before adulthood. Someone is always leaving—a best friend or a favourite teacher—and grief can be experienced even when children leave a place they didn't particularly enjoy; at least it had become familiar and comfortable. It's been said that global nomads go through "hidden funerals." If not dealt with at the time, this grief can build up and emerge later in life.

"It seems that some TCKs believe that acknowledging any pain in their past will negate the joys they have known," note authors Pollock and Van Reken. "Until these TCKs can acknowledge that proper mourning for the inevitable losses in their lives is an affirmation of the richness of the past rather than a negation of the present, they will continue to deny any grief they have felt."

This unacknowledged grief leads to unresolved anger and resentment, especially about a past history that global nomads can't go back and find. Author Anne-Marie MacDonald writes in *The Way the Crow Flies*, her novel about a Canadian military family, "If you move around all your life, you can't find where you come from on a map. All those places where you lived are just that: places. You don't come from any of them: you come from a series of events. Those events are mapped in memory."

All parents want only happy childhood memories for their children, although there are no guarantees that this elusive goal will help their children move into happy adulthoods, mobile or not. Parents raising global nomads, with the unique challenges, numerous transitions, and extraordinary opportunities presented by travel, must be mindful that their job carries an added layer of responsibility from day one.

As the Dalai Lama says in his famous guide for living, *The Art of Happiness*, "A tree with strong roots can withstand the most violent storm, but the tree can't grow roots just as the storm appears on the horizon." It's a wise lesson for expat parents to keep in mind throughout the process of raising their children abroad.

Chapter 2

"WE'RE BEING TRANSFERRED!"

UNLESS MOTHER NATURE is behind it, an earth-shattering, life-altering event doesn't just happen. An overseas assignment, which is not quite as intense as an earth-quake but is nonetheless capable of rocking the ground beneath a family, invariably has a back story. Whether the spouse and family get to hear that story until the move is a done deal may be another matter. I've heard stories of spouses who were informed of a transfer by a relocation agent telephoning to say someone would be right over to do an estimate on packing up their house. Funny, but their husbands forgot to mention anything about a new job abroad before leaving for the office that day.

Anyone who has read my book *A Moveable Marriage* will recall my own story of being blindsided by my husband when he delivered the news that our family was being asked to accept a fourth assignment in Asia, this time to Seoul, South Korea. We were on vacation at the time, just the two of us, so I was more inclined to focus on golf, the beach, and the good Scotch in my hand than on the words coming out of Rodney's mouth. To his credit, he had allowed me a few days to unwind in the sun before breaking it to me that, less than two years after our return to Canada from Beijing, we were being asked to move to Asia again. And oh, yes: we needed to officially accept the offer directly after we returned from holiday.

MAKING THE DECISION TO GO

Whether an employee is being offered an international transfer or an individual decides it would be terrific to move the family abroad for a few years, the groundwork is laid for weeks, months, even years before that can actually happen.

There certainly may have been some hypothetical discussion about moving (the *what if?* conversations). And once the prospect of a move is in play, the family may be presented with the choice of saying no. I personally always found that illogical; if the move was prompted by Rodney's job (which in our case represented our livelihood), and his masters wanted him overseas, I didn't feel there was any real choice in the matter. He was, after all, a diplomat.

Other spouses feel strongly about maintaining some measure of choice. "It's vital to us to make a conscious choice, and always be making these decisions in light of our personal priorities and the best interests of the whole family," one spouse told me. "I also find it really important to have that sense of making the choice and buying into the decision willingly. We always—maybe naïvely—try to remind ourselves that at the end of the day we do have a choice. There is always an alternative, not always the one we would like, but another option nevertheless."

News of a transfer sometimes comes as a pronouncement long after the deal has been sealed. For families who are not normally rotational, the news can leave them

excited but reeling. Even families used to constant relocations may be none too thrilled at the idea of hauling out
the moving cartons again.

Regardless of how the news arrives at the family's
doorstep, though, the quicker everyone gets with the new
program, the happier the family will be.

WHEN TO TELL THE KIDS

Of all of the questions I'm asked on the international lecture circuit, "When should we tell the kids?" is the one
that most regularly pops up (along with its twin, "When
should we move the children home?" I address that thorny
issue later, in a chapter on repatriation challenges).

Your children, especially the teenagers, will probably
figure out something is up long before it becomes official.
They may overhear a telephone call with the movers or
your desperate rant to a sibling or friend. Contractors
may start showing up to fix bits of your house in preparation for its rental. Both parents may be very excited
about the news, and children may catch on to this excite-
ment, guessing the Big Secret before it's allowed to be
revealed. Alternatively, Mommy and Daddy may suddenly be a little tense around each other. Not much eye contact is being made at the dinner table, and when a child
asks if there's anything wrong, a mother may simply hit
her automatic response button: "No, dear, nothing out of
the ordinary." Like heck. What is going on is not the least
bit ordinary.

With all those clues around, most children won't be
surprised when you finally decide to share the news. Still,
I don't think it should be delivered in a casual way—for
instance, in a carload full of their friends on the way to a

soccer practice. An international move is a life-changing event for the entire family, and it should be treated with the respect its magnitude deserves.

Try to make the announcement special. Plan a family meeting so that everyone is together when the news is broken, allowing each family member lots of time to ask questions. The dinner table is a good venue for this event. Make sure *everyone* gets a chance to speak. If children express their anxieties, parents can use the opportunity to let them know they understand those fears.

It's amazing how long the memories of a badly handled relocation announcement can linger. Interculturalist and transition coach Barbara Schaetti turned into a hurt teenager when I asked her to recall how she heard the news of a move her family made from Houston to Singapore during her teenage years. "I remember my father picking me up at my piano lesson to take me home," she said. "I was doing driver's ed at the time, so I thought he was there to allow me to practice driving with him. Instead, he wanted to tell me about a move, which I absolutely did not want to make at that point in my life. I was very angry."

After the news is broken to your whole family and the initial shock has subsided, it's a good idea to engage everyone in the planning stages. Run, don't walk, to a computer and find any one of the thousands of expatriate websites that have information about your future home. Bookmark it for easy access in the coming days and weeks.

One veteran of multiple moves shared another strategy with me: "I'm always careful about the timing of the move, which helps defuse my children's feelings of powerlessness. They may not have a choice about whether or not to move, but if possible, they can have some control over the timing to feel that their needs and wants are respected. So, if my children are already engaged in preparations for something important, like a school production, a music exam (although many kids might happily sacrifice that one!), a special friend's birthday, or an important family occasion or celebration, then we try to honour that."

Be prepared for the proverbial cry of some older children: *You're ruining my life!* Expect some serious sulking or retreats to the bedroom, door slammed on the way in and iPods immediately set to their highest volume. If teenagers are being moved in their last year of high school, be especially sensitive, and give your young adults some time to let the realization sink in that they won't be graduating with their peers. That may be the hardest part for a seventeen-year-old to accept. A college-bound young adult may worry the family is leaving her behind. Young children may often provide comic relief by asking if Santa will be sent a change-of-address card.

If you haven't been consulted by your husband at all, get ready to accept your Academy Award for "Performance by a Mother Pretending to be Thrilled" or your pitch-perfect rendition of what I call the "happy voice." If you present the news to your children with enthusiasm—pointing out the fascinating culture you will be living in, the wonderful holidays you will have, or the delicious food you will eat—this will really help to set a positive tone for your move. You might also remind yourself that, hey, this move could really get your juices flowing if you let go of your anger over not being consulted first. "Finding things to be positive about does not mean ignoring the realities of the move or the new country, but instead recognizing that no experience is all good or all bad, and that overall we can make something of this new opportunity," one mother told me.

Some parents prefer to wait until the last possible moment to tell their children about a transfer. Only you know if this is the best way to proceed with your child. But it's my opinion that you don't do children any favours by delaying the news. If they sense tension in the air, they may think they are the cause of it. And for heaven's sake, don't expect your children not to tell their best friend the news. You've just turned their life upside down. Give them permission to tell at least one other person.

DEALING WITH ANXIETY AND FEAR

Depending on where you are being posted, anticipate a spectrum of your own—and your children's—anxiety and fears to hit you even before the adventure begins. At the simplest end, there will be angst over your child's school, friends, and pets. These three items will top the list of your global nomad's concerns over a pending move. Your own top item might be your fear of the unknown.

In the olden days—that would be fifteen years ago at best—I used to call this kind of insecurity "disaster syndrome." Now, the horrific events we see on the television news are the stuff of nightmares (yours as well as your children's). This has led to a new, stand-alone condition known as "pre-traumatic stress syndrome," in which someone reacts to horrible, devastating events that *might* happen. Dave Pollock first introduced me to this syndrome, which he noted when speaking to children and parents post 9/11. I address this type of fear in more detail later in the book.

By contrast, the most serious concerns for your child will probably be as follows: What will the new school be like? Will I make any new friends? And what about my old ones: will they still remember me? A lot will depend on the age and stage of your child. Preschool children can immediately enter the play group or nursery school circuit in the new location if the mother dives right in and makes connections. But do be prepared for clingy children who don't want to let you out of their sight. Toilet training may move backward too, and thumbs may slide back into mouths for a short while.

I thought we were being clever training our son before he was two not to have to use a diaper during the day. When we moved him from Canada to Taiwan, this meant he qualified for a local nursery school, and I would get a blessed two hours on my own every day. But every morning he would kick and scream when I dropped him off at the school. (My screaming and shouting in the car on the way, as I tried to navigate unfamiliar roads, didn't help matters.) I would slink back home thinking I was the worst mother on earth to have moved him and then, worse, to stash him every morning in a preschool just so I could selfishly write a book. That was until Jay's teacher, one day in passing, reassured me that his crying generally stopped the moment my car was out of sight.

School-age children will have opportunities for new friends from day one of school, but how they adapt will depend on the personality of the child and the social interaction of the parents. The more new friends you make who have kids the same age as yours, the more familiar faces your children will have to reassure them that life does go on. Outgoing children will turn to their neighbours in class or the kid sitting beside them on the school bus and begin an instant friendship. Quiet children may need some help from their parents, especially their mothers. (This may mean hosting the dreaded sleepover as a way of bringing your child into the group.) Some shy children may become glued to the first friendly child to approach them, only to discover a month later that their new friend is a pariah who always gloms onto new kids looking out of place. Like their adult counterparts, your children may find themselves uncomfortably trying to shake friends made too quickly after their arrival.

Friendship for the teenager is a serious business, combining as it does social interaction and the more critical issues of self-image and self-esteem. Making friends is an important part of how teenagers are perceived and accepted. Dismissing their anxiety about it is like dismissing who they are.

Some teens fear a loss of independence—having to travel with and rely on parents again after several years of freedom of movement. Teenagers may be wondering: Does this move mean I have to hang out with my kid sister or brother? Will I be able to shop for my own clothes, or will Mom have to take me? Will I be able to get around on buses? Will I be able to drive? Many anxieties pertaining to teenagers' sense of a separate identity will be spinning around in their heads in the months before the move. Anticipate these fears (and others), and have some solutions and answers ready to discuss.

Many children simply worry about standing out like

a sore thumb in the new location, something you may be able to help with as a parent. Consider this story from a spouse whose family was being posted to Shanghai: "Prior to moving, I sent an e-mail to the [new] school principal, with apologies for asking such banal questions, requesting information about any requirements for school, such as what colour socks the kids were required to wear. We had been given very little in the way of school supply lists and were told all would be provided, including school uniforms. But having a ten-year-old daughter anxious about the move who hates to stand out (unless she chooses to), I knew that turning up on her first day with the wrong colour socks would be something approaching traumatic. I also wanted to buy things like that before we left our home country, when I could get out and find things quickly and easily, rather than in a foreign country, jetlagged, arriving just a few days before school was to start. I felt my overly zealous approach was somewhat vindicated when, a year or so later, in a department store in Shanghai, I was flagged down by an expat mom with several young children in tow, wearing that desperate, almost defeated China-weary look in her eyes, asking whether I could tell her where she could find navy blue socks in children's sizes!"

Reserve final opinions on everything until you see what life is like "over there." But be sure to encourage every member of the family to share how they are feeling. Don't discuss just logistics and practicalities in the days leading up to the move. Honest, open communication about the subject will be more useful in the long run in helping your family to settle into their new home and school.

When I address the notion of "family culture shock"

in the next chapter, I go further down the behavioural road. At this stage (you know you're moving, and it's still a big blur), go easy on how strict you are with your kids about things like clothes left on the floor or shoes and boots left at the door: the little things, in other words, that could cause one of your own predeparture tantrums. At the same time, encourage continuity by keeping to rhythms like mealtimes and bedtimes as well as rituals such as celebrating birthdays or even making beds. Everyone in the family will be riding the same roller coaster of emotions before moving day arrives, and there will be time enough after arrival to reset stricter boundaries and structure in your family's life.

In the meantime, find the website of the school your children will be attending. Many sites show pictures of the campus and highlight activities and sports teams as well as offer a link to the school's parent group. If your husband's company is offering a "look-see" visit to find a house and check out the new city, see if you can visit the school, too. Some parents try to include their children in a preliminary visit, but others counsel against it.

"While it would be great to take your kids along on a look-see, it's neither efficient nor practical, since you might end up tending to their jet lag as well as your own while making major school decisions," an expat spouse posted to Asia told me. "On our look-see trip—without our kids—we took dozens of digital photos of the house we rented, inside and out, as well as those things relevant to the kids' needs and expectations. That included photos of the nearby parks and playgrounds and pictures of the school right down to the classrooms at the time. No detail was too small.

"Our son was very into construction at the time, so we took photos of work sites with tower cranes, excavators, and cement trucks. We gave the kids a big slide show, complete with popcorn, when we returned from our trip, asking them what they thought of everything. It worked really well—the house was a familiar place when they arrived for the first time."

The Internet has been the single greatest invention for global nomads, along with text and instant messaging. These are all ways for your children to keep in touch with their old friends. But rather than just putting cyber tools at their disposal, it's important to constantly reinforce the successes of previous moves or other transitions your children have made in the past, especially in cases where they thought they would be friendless and ended up with a huge crowd of buddies. Your kids may not demonstrate that your encouragement is sinking in, but their inner selves will be getting the message that they have succeeded in the past and can do so again in this new location.

EXPLAINING THE MOVE TO YOUR NEAREST AND DEAREST

Talking about your decision to move overseas with extended family and close friends will be an ongoing challenge throughout your time abroad, but breaking the news is never easy. So many parents have written to me about siblings, grandparents, or friends who simply can't understand why they are moving and whose unhelpful, often hurtful comments can make an already stressful time worse. It can be difficult to ignore comments like "Why don't you stay behind?" I heard such comments before we moved to Seoul, since there were political tensions in the region. Suggestions that I send my husband by himself and essentially break up my family were not what I wanted to hear (even if the thought had crossed my mind).

Grandparents who feel they will never see your little ones are usually the toughest sell on your overseas move. It's true. You *are* moving the grandchildren far away, and possibly to a place where grandparents worry something bad will happen. One of the best ways to deal with grandparents is to plan to have them visit you in your new location, to reassure them as well as to give them a visit with your kids.

Another helpful family exercise is to brainstorm about ways to maintain ongoing contact with grandparents. Tried-and-true methods include using a webcam for virtual face-to-face conversations; setting up a family website where you regularly post pictures; making a homemade DVD of a grandparent reading a bedtime story that children can play before they go to bed; having your children take digital photos to send to their grandparents, and that old standby, sending packages containing children's artwork.

HOW TO HANDLE MOVING DAY

The day the movers arrive can be fraught with emotion for the entire family. That's assuming the entire family is present. Many companies send the employee on ahead, leaving the spouse to organize everything from the renting out of the house to the farewell parties to the packing up and the long journey to the new home.

Opinion is divided on the subject of whether or not children should watch the movers take their lives out of the house in boxes. There's no denying that packing is easier without little ones underfoot, so if you have very young children, now is the time to call in favours from friends or family and park your children somewhere else for the day. Schoolchildren will typically be out of the house when the movers come to load up, but it's my opinion that children should see the empty house before leaving the country to make it real. Little ones especially may daydream that their house is standing just as they left it, and when they get homesick (as they will in the early days), they will think they can go back and find nothing has changed. Family therapist Lois Bushong highly recommends walking preschoolers through the house or yard and bidding things good-bye. I remember with much nostalgia waving good-bye to Bangkok with two-year-old Lilly as the plane took off. The two of us were headed for Canada while her father stayed behind.

There are all sorts of ways to engage your children in the moving process, beginning with their own rooms and with travel bags they can fill with their favourite things for the journey. When my children were very young and our shipments went partly by air but mostly by sea, I made sure the contents of their rooms went the quicker air route so that those boxes could be unpacked first and a familiar setting (their bedrooms) could magically re-appear overseas. I even used to take my son's favourite pillowcase onto the airplane, just to have something familiar on hand.

It's hard to know which of your belongings to take and which to leave behind. I always recommend that anything you couldn't bear to lose in a move (precious silver inherited from a grandmother, for instance) should stay in the home country in storage. Pictures and everything else that adorned your home to make it cozy should definitely be brought along.

Put important documents such as birth certificates and immunization and school records in your carry-on luggage. If you think you will be able to just fish them out of your shipment when it arrives, you will be in for a shock when your household goods get stuck at customs or on a slow boat somewhere. What you pack for the plane trip will depend entirely on whether you prefer to travel light or heavy.

TRAVELING WITH CHILDREN

Every mother works out a strategy for traveling with her children. Note that I say mother: so often the mother must travel alone with the children because her husband has gone ahead to begin work. Entire books have been published on the subject of traveling alone with children (see the resources section at the back of the book), so I'll offer just a few choice pieces of advice.

I can't remember how I came up with the idea of a "magic bag," but it got me back and forth across the Pacific with my kids so many times that I absolutely guarantee it. Each child gets to buy a new knapsack for the journey. In it, everything they could conceivably want or need to distract them is wrapped up individually, like presents. Who cares that a crayon or an apple juice container has a bow on it? You have no idea how many times I've used the "Let's go to the magic bag now" routine to keep a child amused. After spending way too much money on new toys and then discovering that a paper cup or airplane window shade could be just as amusing, I nixed buying anything except new books or playing cards. But the magic bag, with its seemingly endless supply of little presents, was indeed magical in its effect. One key piece of advice for parents traveling with very young children: pack two of everything precious to them, and that means an extra pacifier!

When it comes to food, order ahead for children's meals or bring your own, which is the way most airlines are going now anyway. Even if you plan to buy food on the plane, your child usually wants to eat or drink something way before the cart goes through, so come prepared with a small pantry in your own magic bag.

I never pre-boarded with my children, but this is a matter of personal preference. I found we didn't need an extra half-hour in which they could rip open things or read new books before we had even left the gate. Of course, with babies you'll likely need the extra time to settle in.

If you've ever traveled alone with kids, you probably won't have trouble inserting yourself into this all-too-common story shared by an Australian wife: "I did the long-haul flight from our home in the U.S. to Singapore on my own, with an eleven-month-old in tow, when I was nearly eleven weeks pregnant and vomiting three times a day with morning sickness. That flight alone nearly killed me. I remember lying on the cabin floor at 2:00 a.m. not able to move, having just vomited up my entire dinner in the toilet, with my eleven-month-old sleeping twenty feet from me in a bassinet and the cabin purser rifling through my hand luggage, trying to find my anti-nausea pills, so that I could at least stand up and go back to my seat and die a slow death there instead of on the cabin floor. Looking back on it, it was a nightmare! But I survived (with a lot of resentment towards my husband)."

Don't forget to teach your children airplane manners. Do this sooner rather than later. I found that having well-behaved children (all right, sometimes I wanted to put them in the overhead bins) gained me a lot of brownie points with fellow travelers.

Try to arrange for someone to greet you at the airport upon arrival (preferably your husband). There is nothing worse than getting into a strange airport late at night, with kids and luggage (and maybe the dog that has accompanied you), not knowing a word of the local language, and then searching for a cab. For someone in a jet-lagged, exhausted state, this scenario can definitely be the proverbial straw that breaks the camel's back.

If you are going to be put up in a hotel for a few days or weeks before your house is ready, try to arrange for someone (your moving company or the spouse of a new colleague) to fill your hotel fridge with something for the little ones to eat until you can find a nearby convenience or grocery store. These kinds of touches can set the tone right off the bat for a healthy and positive arrival.

A FEW FINAL WORDS OF ADVICE

We often paper over our children's relocation challenges with reminders of how lucky they are to be moving abroad. That may be, but their childhood or adolescent concerns—like acceptance at a new school or by new friends, or having to leave a pet behind—are just as important to them as your job or your new house is to you. Be available to them as much as possible during this transition period. If tears flow once in a while, that's all right, too. Children need to be allowed to *feel* their emotions without a parent's constant intellectualizing.

Consider this wise advice posted on a chat group on my website for mobile families: "If only we could remember that the outcomes are a success when we are in the midst of the turmoil." Soon after it was posted (by a mother guilt-ridden about moving her child away from home), another member of the chat group chimed in with her thanks: "Your message came at a great time for me as this is our first assignment and so every step is a new experience in emotion." This mother of three children, all under the age of five, was about to pack up for an overseas assignment. She continued: "Two things happened during these past two days to remind me there's nothing really accidental. First, your post came along with a strong 'everything ends up better than you expect' message. And secondly, a neighbour whom I had never met knocked on my door yesterday. She saw the overseas container sitting in front of our home. She then gushed about how much she had loved her three overseas assignments, how her kids had not just done well with the moves but were better people for it, and on and on. Talk about timing!"

Chapter 3

MOVING THROUGH CULTURE SHOCK

"MOM, DOES FLYING on an airplane make a dog go bald?"

Jay, seven years old at the time, was taking a momentary breather from sobbing at the sight of our almost hairless family pet Sandy, a handsome young Shetland sheepdog, to pose this intriguing question.

Sandy looked even worse than I did after our eleven-hour flight over the Pacific to our new home in Seoul. That's saying a lot, considering the state of my own wild, curly hair, but at least mine was still attached to my head. Sandy was lying *on* his gold and white coat. Cowering inside his travel cage, he was skinny, thirsty-looking and obviously shell-shocked.

Lilly's eyes had been welled up with distress for most of the endless journey. She was fretting that her beloved dog had been relegated to the cold cargo hold of the 747. Seeing Sandy's empty water dish, still attached to the cage but upside down and dry as a bone, completely undid her after we deplaned. We had lovingly placed ice cubes in his bowl before our departure from Vancouver airport, following the sensible advice given to us by people who specialize in transporting expat pets abroad. The ice, we were told, would melt en route and keep Sandy supplied with cool refreshment. No one had bothered to mention that if the dish were to tip over (which it obviously had done), all the liquid would be gone. Our pooch had also boarded drug free, to avoid having him wake up somewhere over the ocean and wonder if he were in doggie hell. By the look of him, his canine radar was telling him now that he had not landed in heaven.

EVEN PETS EXPERIENCE CULTURE SHOCK

Rodney and I were mostly grateful to have finally *found* Sandy after a byzantine late-night arrival that was enough to make anyone's stress levels go off the chart. Sandy, it had certainly seemed at first, was destined to become a piece of lost luggage.

We had circled endlessly around the airport searching for our dog. Our official Canadian embassy greeter told us Sandy would be brought to us outside the luggage hall. We exited only to discover we actually needed to be back inside. But once we were there, Sandy was nowhere to be found. Rodney fumed, the children cried, and I tried to figure out a way to sneak a cigarette, even though I had just quit smoking *again*. I was embarrassed that Rodney made no effort to disguise his irritation, which he expressed at the top of his lungs, to everyone from the Air Canada staff to the Korean airport officials. So much for diplomatic aplomb. Up and down the airport we charged, our luggage carts overflowing, looking like a crazy family in a bad Steve Martin movie. Like complete idiots, we started calling Sandy's name, as if the dog would hear us and, Houdini-like, manage to escape from his traveling cage. Fortunately, the airport had emptied out, so there was no audience for our lunacy. But we still didn't have our dog.

And then, by some miracle, Sandy was found. That was the good news. The bad news, as noted by our son, was that our dog's hair had fallen out. And the news got worse: South Korean rules dictated that Sandy go into quarantine for ten days. My children would not rest until they had personally inspected the place where their dog would be housed. So off we went to the quarantine facility, in a direction toward the infamous Demilitarized Zone (the highly dangerous and heavily guarded DMZ, at a time when saber rattling between North and South Korea had been making ominous headlines). We watched our lovely pet stare back at us from between the bars of a military truck driving directly in front of us. It could not have been more surreal. If Sandy could have spoken, I'm sure he would have demanded to know why the hell he wasn't in our van with the rest of us.

KIDS REMEMBER THE GLITCHES

As parents, we always want things to go smoothly. What sticks out in a child's mind—whether related to travel, a new home or school, or the huge fight that Mommy and Daddy had—is everything that's gone wrong. Years later, our entire family well remembers this story about Sandy, especially as it ended with the four of us sharing a giant bed in the presidential suite of the Grand Hyatt Seoul because we had arrived too late from the quarantine facility to claim the rooms we had reserved.

Despite all the tears at the time, the retelling of our crazy first night in Seoul always produces tons of laughter. And that's something positive to keep in mind: there *is* an upside to life seemingly turning upside down. Your children will remember these stories forever.

RELAX, IT'S JUST EXHAUSTION!

Only years later did I come to understand how the utter exhaustion caused by the journey to a new posting (and all the moving preparations and farewell parties that precede it) contributes to a family's collective hysteria on arrival. Who really sleeps on airplanes? On our way to Seoul, for instance, the kids managed to sleep—as children always do, sometimes perversely, in the last twenty minutes of a long flight—but I had dozed only intermittently, if at all. With no rest, and the anxiety of our possibly lost pet, no wonder the four of us on arrival had tempers one step away from exploding. Who had the strength to cope with anything?

In the first twenty-four hours after arrival at a new posting, I believe parents suffer less from culture shock (which hasn't had a chance to kick in yet) and more from being wiped out. Many mothers face the additional stress of their husband being out of town when the family arrives. Remember, though, that your children look to their parents, and especially you, their mother, as their Rock of Gibraltar. Try not to crumble in front of them. Find the nearest washroom and melt down privately.

WHAT IS CULTURE SHOCK, ANYWAY?

The term "culture shock" was coined in the early 1950s by anthropologist Kalvero Oberg to describe the feelings human beings experience when they travel to or live in a different country or culture. It is the original "fish out of water" tale.

Culture shock has very distinct stages. It begins like all good things do, with a *honeymoon period*. Like a tourist visiting a new country, you will find everything and everyone interesting and enchanting at the beginning. In the early days abroad, in fact, the similarities between cultures are often more obvious than the differences. For example, you might have arrived at a slick, modern airport, grabbed a Starbucks latte to go, and jumped into a taxi with a driver who's talking on a cell phone, can accept a computerized VISA payment, and has GPS to make sure he doesn't get lost. What's to be shocked about? It's just like home!

Until that driver turns to you and says "$##$#@*&!"—which in his language, the one you don't yet speak or understand, could mean anything. The *crisis stage* of culture shock has begun. During this stage, frustration and anger may consume family members. Everything is foreign, no longer exotic, and totally exasperating. You're mad that things are so different, but it's not always clear where to direct your anger. During the crisis stage, your children will definitely be mad at you, the parent. Don't take it personally. The employer typically gets the bulk of a family's anger. "Why weren't we told about this?" is a common refrain.

Phase three of culture shock, the *flight stage,* comes when running away from it all—or desperately wanting to—seems like a viable option. This is usually the time when your children start asking to go home.

If running away is not an option, then hiding out can seem like the perfect alternative solution. For a depressed mother, this may be the time when a cozy bed duvet covers up her discontent and muffles the sounds of unhappy children. The bed may also provide a warm place to hide out while the kids trash the new house and you let them. (You may actually want to join in.) I certainly was known to pull the bedcovers over my head at the beginning of our relocations, and I'm apparently the expert. Depending on their age, children will either cling to their mothers during this stage or surgically insert the earbuds of an iPod, taking them out only to answer their cell phones.

One expat mother jokingly calls the flight stage of the culture shock she experienced on her first move abroad as the gift that kept on giving. "I would be fine until one of the kids came down with a mystery illness," she wrote to me. "I would have had zero confidence in the doctor we went to for treatment. Or until my husband came home catastrophically late for the zillionth time in a row. I was completely undone and would want to leave the post—as if packing up the house I had just set up and hauling the kids on a seventeen-hour trip to move in with relatives would fix everything! Basically, it would creep up on me when something went wrong and I would have to talk myself down by saying things like 'It's not this place, it's just *life* that's happening here.' Things go wrong no matter where you are."

Magically, all the crossed wires—in your head as well as in your home—eventually get untangled. You reconnect with yourself and your surroundings. It may have taken an entire year's worth of holidays and milestones like birthdays and anniversaries, but culture shock exits the room and lets you begin your new life.

The one-year estimate is just that, an estimate. Some people breeze through culture shock in record time. Do be aware, though, that everyone feels culture shock in one way or another, and every family member will experience it differently.

CULTURE SHOCK IN THE DIGITAL WORLD

New technologies have had a major impact on the way the traditional stages of culture shock play out. Technology can, in fact, delay the process of working through these stages in order to come out the other side.

In the early stages of your transition, the Internet and cell phones can be a lifesaver for parents. An American spouse living in Korea with young children told me she was grateful when, soon after arrival, her new caregiver, using her own cell phone, connected her with a local play group. A local chatroom helped this spouse discover the next meeting of a women's club as well as find information on much-needed goods and services. When used locally, digital connections can be immensely helpful.

When the messaging goes global, though, a false sense of connection is enhanced. This can be especially true for children who are text messaging or chatting online with friends back home. Adults, too, with family and old friends just an easy click away, may falsely feel rooted in communities that are not nearby.

These types of connections—as comforting as they may be—are nevertheless virtual. They are not happening in real time in a family's new real world. A lot of e-mail is done while wearing a bathrobe. Would anyone go out to meet new people wearing their pajamas? Distracting yourself by sitting at a computer "talking" with a friend thousands of miles away may fill the day, but it can create a dreamlike state that won't help you settle into your new locale.

One longtime French expat spouse, a veteran of multiple overseas moves, wrote to me from Indonesia that while her family enjoys the expat network they have built and maintained via the Internet, she believes cautionary words about e-mail should be offered to any family moving abroad. "E-mail contact probably has some bad sides to it," she wrote. "The contact is great, but it can postpone the time when we actually feel settled. E-mail contact can be artificial and move us away from settling down where we are actually living."

Barbara Schaetti agrees. In her work as a transition coach for expatriate families, she has seen the Internet become a hindrance rather than a facilitator when people rely on absent friends and family to the exclusion of peers in the new locale. It is the crisis stage of culture shock that has the biggest potential to be affected, Schaetti says.

"During the honeymoon phase, you're out in your new location checking things out, seeing all the commonalities. Your reports home are likely to be relatively happy ones, and you're not as likely to be glued to the computer waiting for a response as when you're feeling miserable and miserably misunderstood. But when people are in the crisis or flight stages, they're less likely to leap away from their computer, given the illusory appeal it offers of home community connection. Cultural learning won't happen, and they could get stuck in the crisis stage of culture shock. And without cultural learning," asks Schaetti, "why bother to have packed up your house and family in the first place? If there's no gain, it sure isn't worth the pain!"

Children raised on text messaging, instant messaging, and cell phones may have a hard time breaking the digital umbilical cord with home or their last posting. As parents, you naturally want your children to breeze happily through the early days of relocation. If communicating with friends back home pacifies them, it's hard to take that away. But a friend over the computer or a cell phone is not a friend in the here and now.

A fellow Canadian spouse, another veteran of multiple moves around the world, thinks e-mail is "both a godsend and a curse, allowing the family to stay in touch with their friends but definitely hampering the settling-in process." She recounted a particularly difficult time with her then fifteen-year-old daughter, who fell in love four weeks before the family was moving halfway around the world.

"She carried the virtual relationship on for months, making both herself and the rest of the family miserable," this spouse remembers. "As mothers, we sometimes have to resort to extremes, and having access to her e-mails, I was able to at least figure out that this fellow was not a good influence and that her histrionics over him were mainly for effect. Even so, our sensitive child once again pushed us to the limits. This would have been the case regardless of a move or not, but it's more difficult to find support when you are in unfamiliar territory and your husband is out of town most of the time."

Take care to see that your children balance the old and the new. Don't let their technological toys prevent them from working through the stages of culture shock and, ultimately, from integrating into their new surroundings.

Remember, cross-cultural experiences, growth, and the making of new friends simply won't happen in a cyber bubble. "The more that bubble segregates you from your new cultural environment, the less meaningful ultimately your sojourn will be. It may feel safer at the time, but there's nothing like regrets for missed opportunities upon repatriation," advises Barbara Schaetti. And those missed opportunities may have long-term ramifications. "There will be all the grief and anger at what was given up (family, friends, career, known world) without any of the appreciation for what was gained, because what was there to be gained was missed altogether or not maximized as it could have been."

GRIEF PLAYS A ROLE IN CULTURE SHOCK

Few people are willing to shout this news out loud, but culture shock and grief are closely connected. It's rare to find culture shock workshops that focus on themes of loss as they relate to relocation, and there's a good reason for that: Would families really want to leave home if they thought they were headed into a period of mourning instead of an exciting adventure?

As I've stressed in the past and will continue to stress in the future, for most families, the eventual outcome of a move abroad is a positive, enriching, and often life-altering experience. But any skeptic who thinks relocation is not related to grief should take a quick stroll around a bookstore. Most books examining the subject place relocation high on the list of life events that can trigger grief, along with more obvious major events such as death and divorce.

Culture shock is driven at the outset by multiple losses. These vary depending on your life stage and family configuration, but they include leaving behind family, friends, familiar surroundings, and, for many accompanying spouses, careers.

Unlike with the death of a loved one, however, there are no rituals for the grief experienced by expats. On the contrary, mourning the loss of home and acting out homesickness by walking around a new city or school playground looking dazed, confused, and unhappy is considered by many expats to be somehow "letting the side down." Everyone is supposed to just get on with it, the sooner the better. Experts call this "disenfranchised grief" and believe that, if not expressed, it can inhibit a child's development.

A macho denial of the culture shock experience persists nonetheless. If there is one common thread to the many conversations I have had with expat parents over the years, it is this popular response to my inquiry about culture shock: "Who, me? I never had culture shock. And my children adapted perfectly. We all took it in without any problems whatsoever." I tell the story often of women I've met who maintain they have suffered no culture shock but are consuming their third or fourth gin and tonic of the evening.

Confessing to culture shock is somehow seen as admitting to failure rather than as a validation of the normal, healthy experience it is. The denial is fueled by everything from ego to the position the family has in the expat community or the company. For some people, everything has to look picture-perfect. But to deny the grief of culture shock is to push the problem aside. One day there will be a reckoning.

That's because grief does not just magically disappear. Time on its own does not always heal, according to Elva Mertick, a Calgary-based grief counselor and family therapist who prepares expats both going abroad and coming home to Canada's oil patch. Mertick firmly believes it's what you *do* with this time that makes the difference. Loss creates an emotional wound, she says. People need to work actively at their grief in order to recover. An exciting new expatriate life can emerge only once all the stages of grief—shock, denial, anger, bargaining, depression, and acceptance—are acknowledged. Do those stages sound familiar? They ought to, as they are essentially the phases of culture shock.

WHAT IS FAMILY CULTURE SHOCK?

Family culture shock is an often overlooked form of the phenomenon. It is a *collective* experience of loss: the loss of control over new surroundings and, later, over each other's behaviour. As each individual family member struggles in their own way with the shock of regaining equilibrium, that person's behaviour and moods can deeply affect others in the family. This may be exacerbated by the constant physical and emotional proximity the family experiences in the early weeks after arrival.

Children, for example, may be in a pleasant honeymoon stage of finding everything about the new place really cool. They are happy. Then they go to school, hate it immediately or find it scary, and come home in a terrible mood, determined not to go back the next day. Byebye honeymoon, hello crisis. Meanwhile, the mother may have, as I habitually did, skipped the honeymoon and gone straight into crisis, while trying to find schools, post office, grocery stores, and other key places. The minute the kids got onto the school bus, though, she kicked back and had her first good day in her new location. Until the children came home in tears—children of *all* ages.

Dad, for his part, has not been around much during the settling in, and he arrives home one evening from a business trip with all of his own complaints. Of course, his rant will occur just as the rest of the family is talking about a terrific restaurant nearby that they all enjoyed. His mood brings the house down.

Says therapist Lois Bushong: "The move can upset how the family relates to one another. As in any crisis, it takes time for a family to re-stabilize. And more than just time, honest communication with one another, flexibility, and the ability to sit back and laugh about it will be very helpful."

A CHILD'S VIEW OF CULTURE SHOCK

A child's culture shock in a new home in a foreign country can be a complex matter. Parents often overlook the fact that children need time to adjust to not only different weather, food, people on the street, classrooms, and playgrounds, but also to new family dynamics, which may include changes in their parents' behaviour.

From a child's perspective, the shock may appear to be traceable to their father, who is often away, either at the office or on a business trip, or is constantly on his computer or cell phone. This may be nothing new—their father might have worked like that in the home culture, too. But now, in this new environment, children want him around more, even if it's just to keep him in their sight. Conversely, if their father had a lot more time to devote to them before he took the international assignment, children may be keenly feeling the loss of him in their daily life. Their mother, meanwhile, stressed from setting up the household on her own, may be finding it difficult to disguise her unhappiness.

Language barriers may surface early, depending on where the family has relocated. Your husband may speak the local language because he was offered language training. Children, as is often the case, may learn the language from the playground or the street, then have parents depend on them to do the translating. This is similar to the immigrant experience. Yet it is you, the mother, who is trying to get everything organized for everyone. Trying to get a lightbulb changed was once the litmus test of frustration in a foreign country. Now, with so much home technology to be hooked up, frustration levels have increased exponentially. Your fuse may grow short with the kids.

In the first few weeks and months after arrival in a foreign country, it is unquestionably the mother who experiences the most jolts to her existence. Her roles (at home, in her marriage, in the new foreign community) change the most dramatically. Her day is unstructured, whereas her husband goes off to his new office and her children start up in the controlled environment of a new school. If the children are not yet of school age, she may also be dealing with a local caregiver of whom she has little sense due to language and culture barriers.

To some children (I recall my own feeling this way) it may seem that different parents came out of the moving boxes. Who are these screaming monsters, and why is Mommy crying all the time?

Children are innocent bystanders to their parents' marital adjustments during the transition phase. At the same time, they have to cope with their own reactions to the new country, new house, and new school, and maybe to the absence of a beloved pet who wasn't allowed to come. They don't understand a word of the language at first, either, and they are often left with babysitters with whom they can't communicate. Until the new environment becomes the reality, the picture will seem slightly out of focus.

When we were living in Beijing, I came home one day near the beginning of our assignment to hear, even before I opened the door, three-year-old Jay screaming. He was yelling from behind the bathroom door while on the other side our caregiver, or *ayi,* laughed and clapped her hands. He was screaming "Let me out of here!" while she laughed, thinking it was a game, because neither of them understood the other. When I finally rescued my son (and I'm not sure who was the biggest basket case, him or me), I called up our embassy and had them remove every lock on every door inside the apartment.

A CHILD'S CULTURE SHOCK IS DIFFERENT

A child's culture shock may not seem that much different from an adult's. It's an initial reaction to an uncertain and different environment. But never forget that your traveling child is not just a miniature adult. A child is, after all, a child, with needs that can't be put on hold, as an adult's can.

Children experience things in a much more emotional way, according to Priscila Montana, a longtime cross-cultural trainer who runs the Dallas-based company Cultural Awareness International. "I feel there is a greater sense of loss and disorientation for children when they move. Unlike their parents, they are quite unfamiliar with what is happening and where they are going. The unknown is frightening to them. I have even often heard younger children ask: 'Will I ever see Grandma again?' " says Montana.

A child's shock may mimic an adult's but with one key difference: children lack the verbal skills to express their feelings or, if they are teenagers, may choose not to activate their verbal skills as a way of demonstrating their displeasure over the move. That's why it helps when parents provide the words.

"Not only do words capture the meaning of the situation, but they also help a child accept their feelings as being normal," one longtime American foreign service spouse told me. During one of her family's numerous transitions, one of her younger children was starting to worry about every little thing. So finally she said to him: "Perhaps you aren't used to all this new stuff yet." He picked up on that expression right away. It seemed to be what he was looking for, and it became his mantra for coping. "Mom," he would say to her in a strange situation that might have unsettled him at first, "I'm just not used to this yet!"

Children will use behaviour (not always their best, either) to express themselves during the early stages of culture shock. And since they are acute observers and easily pick up cues, attitudes, and behaviour from their parents, remember to watch what you say around them. During the most difficult transition of our lives, to a posting in Taiwan, I'm afraid I introduced my two-year-old son to a very colourful vocabulary, which he would spout in perfect imitation of me from the backseat of our car. I learned to put a zipper on my frustration.

STRATEGIES TO COUNTER ASPECTS OF CULTURE SHOCK

Regardless of children's age or stage of development, there are some universal stressors that will trigger culture shock for them. Here they are, along with some strategies for combating them.

• *Loss of the familiar*

I wrote at great length in my earlier book, *A Parent's Guide*, about the shock our son felt after moving from our rural Canadian home in western Quebec, where a meadow of wildflowers grew in the summer and snowy hills were close at hand for sledding in the winter, to polluted, congested Taipei. He screamed for six months before calming down. It didn't help that his parents had been replaced by a seething, resentful mother who was trying to write her first book and a father who was struggling to learn Mandarin.

It's important to recreate, as quickly as possible, something familiar for your young children in your new home, as this mother's story illustrates: "When we made our last move, my husband and I were keen to get out and explore the many local cafés and taverns on weekends. Our children, though, started begging us to go home and have chicken and fresh rolls for Sunday lunch. This had been our standard lunch during the three years we lived in our home culture between assignments, where it was a convenient option that fitted our lifestyle at that time. We would often walk home from church via the local shops and pick up some fresh bread, a roast chicken, and some fresh fruit and vegetables. At home, it would all be put on the table for an easy, do-it-yourself lunch. So we did that for them in our new location, and it made me realize their desire to return to the simple Sunday lunch was probably about more than just the food on the table."

The familiar things may be bedroom furniture, photos, bed linen, or an army of stuffed toys. Do what you can to make your children feel that, despite the scenery outside the door having shifted dramatically, they have a safe little cave in which to hide, and some family routines or rituals that don't change.

• *Loss of friends*
Friends are everything to children. Friends offer validation, support, and a feeling of acceptance. Feeling left out will make your kids awkward and unsure of themselves at a time in their lives when self-consciousness is already second nature. Try not to be dismissive by saying things like "Oh, you'll make all sorts of new friends," when that has not happened yet. Kids don't know if they will make new friends, and you have to respect that fear. But you can also help move things along. I've known mothers who have gone out into the street and knocked on the doors of houses where they saw young children enter. As I mentioned earlier, you may also need to help your children make new friends by inviting other kids to sleepovers or family get-togethers.

• *Language barriers and unfamiliar customs*
It's helpful, if you have younger children, to find caregivers who can speak more than a few words of your own language. But unfamiliar customs can also be a child's undoing, and this can be as simple as being touched all the time or the culture's attitude toward school. But the potential shock of new cultural customs can be turned

into tremendous pleasure by approaching these as a wonderful by-product of life in the new country.

This is an adventure, so get out there and explore. Shop at a local market, for instance. Spicy, unfamiliar-looking food may spark feelings of alienation in a child. "What is that glop that woman is eating, Mom?" "What is that person selling, Dad?" "What has the cook put on my plate? Do I have to eat it?" When children can remember the kind vendor they bought the ingredients from, however, or are coaxed into tasting something they had previously stated they would never eat, it's amazing how this helps them settle in.

• *A new school*
I explore the shocks of a new school in detail in chapter 6. For now, just recognize that a new school is a guaranteed flash point for kids. It can be a very scary place at first (not that older teens will admit this). All school-age children know there are "in" and "out" places to eat lunch, hang out in, and so on; and until your kids learn where those places are, they may feel overwhelmed. Children also need to learn the school "road map," so they know where the bus leaves from, where the gym and the bathrooms are, where their classroom is located, and more. This process takes time, and while they are learning the ropes, they may feel disoriented and insecure. Fortunately, children have a much better sense of direction in new places than do adults.

Since my children were often the new ones in schools as they grew up, I taught them from a very early age to keep an eye open for those children with a "lost look" in their eyes. "Remember when that was you?" I would teach them. "Go over and give them a hand." I do believe in the "what goes around comes around" way of living, and your kids will benefit from other mothers out there teaching their children the same lesson.

• *Household help and status issues*
Families moving to countries where household help will be available will also have the culture shock of people doing everyday things for them. As I wrote in *A Parent's Guide*, on the one hand, helpers may be a dream come true for a young boy or girl—"You mean I don't have to straighten up my room? I don't have to clear the dinner dishes? Take out the garbage?" On the other hand, a child in the throes of this new domestic ecstasy may be brought down to earth when his parents tell him he now has more time for homework or practicing the piano. Older children may mistake a houseful of helpers or business-class tickets or five-star resort holidays as a sign of elevation in family social status or finances. The rank the father holds in a government operation, the military, a company, or a media outlet will have a fallout effect on children. If they aren't used to the perks, this can colour their perception of reality.

The impact on *parents* of this newfound elevated status can also be discombobulating. If parents want their children to keep their feet on the ground, they'll need to plant their own feet firmly in place. Remember that back home, there will be no chauffeur or invitations to gala balls.

WHICH CHILDREN ARE MOST SUSCEPTIBLE TO CULTURE SHOCK?
I will stress this again: everyone experiences culture shock in some way. Children from a few particular groups, however, can be singled out for special mention.

• *First-timers*

If living abroad is a brand-new experience for a family, so too will be the experience of culture shock. Families may have traveled on holiday to a foreign country, but spending two weeks in a resort town is not the same as setting up a household and going to school. The family moving abroad for the first time is naturally more prone to stronger feelings of disorientation and alienation.

"Most first-timers quickly become indistinguishable from veterans of the expatriate life, but until they do, they struggle," I wrote in *A Parent's Guide*. This still holds true. At first, parents are in the dark about what to expect, so they can't advise their children in any experienced way. And even if they do feel something strange is going on, they may deny it. Nobody wants to admit to not handling adjustment well. Everyone wants to be settled in now, not later. But unrealistic expectations like these will only delay adaptation.

• *Children of working parents*

When I helped out with that Brownie troop in Beijing, I could tell immediately which little girls were the offspring of dual-career marriages and which weren't. This is not to say that children of stay-at-home mothers don't have their own issues. And among expats, one is hard-pressed to find someone who actually does stay at home, since expat life can be extraordinarily busy. I raise this point only to say that the children who didn't have at least one parent around for a good chunk of time—the father will do nicely if his spouse is the breadwinner—were desperately seeking my attention during those Brownie meetings. They were not getting the attention they needed at home.

• *Sensitive children*

Having raised one sensitive child and one easily transferable child, I can tell you from firsthand experience that sensitive children have a hard time adjusting to international moves. If you have a child who is very sensitive to change, be ready to battle culture shock for a much longer time. These children want to be rooted, and they find it exceedingly difficult each time they must leave friends or family. These are the children who will tell you they are *positive* they will not make any new friends in the new place.

• *Children of cross-cultural marriages*

Children of mixed-culture marriages are susceptible to a particular form of culture shock. Perhaps an American father and a European mother move away from the United States, exposing their children for the first time to the mother's extended family and birth culture. A child who fits into the new culture visually but has no language capabilities will also find it difficult to adjust. Fortunately for children of cross-cultural marriages, most international schools have a high percentage of enrollments from this group. These children will quickly find others with whom they can compare notes.

HOW DO YOU KNOW IF YOUR CHILD IS EXPERIENCING CULTURE SHOCK?

Physical symptoms are often the most obvious clue that your child is suffering from culture shock. A child who tosses and turns through sleepless nights and emerges in the morning with dark circles under his eyes is clearly having trouble adjusting. Headaches and an upset stomach are other indicators, especially if these mean the child gets to stay home from school. Crying may be another sign that adaptation is not going smoothly. (Crying suddenly and without any apparent cause can certainly be tied to unhappiness, but it may also be attributable to jet lag in the early days.) When a child is tired and not eating well, there is no telling how he will react to things. Don't let the situation go on too long without having a conversation to see if you can find out what is upsetting your child. Young children may tend to visit the nurse's office a lot at the beginning of a new school year while they are settling in. There can also be a higher number of minor mishaps in the playground, which call for reassurance from parents as much as they do for a band-aid.

It can be easier to spot a toddler's culture shock. Just when the mother needs a nap in the most desperate way herself, a young child will decide it's time to give up naps. Your child may also start clinging to you for dear life, even though she demonstrated some independence before the move. She's not taking any chances now. Similarly, a toilet-trained toddler may suddenly become untrained, a young boy may start sucking his thumb again, or a preschooler may refuse to let go of her bottle. All of them are clinging to familiar lifelines as a means of ensuring their parents' attention.

For some young children, the onset of culture shock may be delayed. As one mother living in Asia told me about her five-year-old son, "Initially, he seemed to be handling the move very well. But he rebounded into culture shock after the return from our summer home leave. Reports of his altered behaviour at school were a clue for us, but also, he refused to be in a different room from me while at home."

Some children can be terribly fearful of being left with babysitters in strange surroundings. Knowing that a parent is on speed dial on a cell phone may be reassuring, but in the early days, before you have your new phone accounts set up or know a neighbour who can be contacted in an emergency, try not to go out too much without your kids. Your children may be terrified that you will not come back. I met a young boy once who demanded to see his parents' passports before they went out for the evening; he was fearful they were slipping out of the country, not just going out to dinner.

Nightmares can be the flip side of insomnia for kids experiencing culture shock. The child eventually falls asleep only to dream about fiery plane crashes, torture by teachers, or equally graphic interactions with his new culture. If this is happening, turn off your television.

Finally, never forget the anger a child who has been uprooted may be feeling. She may be powerless to express that anger to you, her parents, but she can hit the child sitting next to her on the school bus or standing on the playground. Watch for anger to be released in other ways by young children, such as throwing their toys around.

HELPING THE FAMILY MOVE THROUGH CULTURE SHOCK

Just about everyone gets through culture shock eventually. If you can maintain perspective and a good sense of humour, the fog will lift and life will be smooth sailing again. But parents should be ready to face some tough days for at least three to six months, and often as long as one year. That is the average time of what culture shock experts call the "period of readjustment." During that period, remember the following tips:

• *Make one parent available at the beginning.*
Limit your socializing in the first few weeks after your family's arrival. It always helped in my family that I *abhor* cocktail parties. (I hate to get dressed up, if truth be told.) One of us (and that would be me) would always offer to stay home. You and your husband need to get out on your own, too, but make it a reasonable amount of time that you spend away from your children in the early days. I've met parents who go out every evening in their newfound role as socialites abroad. This puts way too much stress on the kids. If the working partner simply has to make an appearance at a business party, he can go alone. As the mother, don't allow yourself to be pressured into doing anything but putting your child's welfare first.

• *Create structure and stability.*
In the next chapter, I wade deep into the subject of boundaries and limits. In the years since I wrote my first parenting book, a world of "parenting without borders" has sprung up. But children need limits, and they need structure; the two should go hand in hand after a relocation. A stable home environment will provide the security in which young children can flourish and allow all of you to better enjoy the new host culture.

Routines encourage stability, so, as quickly as possible, establish a new family-life rhythm. You can be strict without cutting off amusements entirely. You are still the boss in your home; there are still house rules and assignments. Be consistent, but be more flexible, too. The larger lesson for children to learn is that survival in another culture often depends on a person's ability to bend a little and to cultivate understanding, patience, and tolerance.

• *Don't let your own prejudices show.*
When you first arrive and things go wrong, it's easy to blame the local culture. Nobody can stay totally cool, especially a frazzled mother trying to unpack a shipment, when the electricity goes off or two dozen workmen sent over by the moving company are trying to drop your piano. (I'm not making that one up.) If your children see you lose your cool in the heat of the moment and scream at a local person, at least ensure they hear your subsequent apology. I certainly made my share of after-the-tantrum phone calls.

• *Control the use of technology.*
When used in a constructive and healthy way, technology is a fantastic tool for the entire family. But parents should keep a close eye on their children, especially in the early months when culture shock will be at its highest levels. As I'm quick to point out to men addicted to their BlackBerry, there actually is an "off" button.

In the days of the British Raj in India, children were referred to as "outposts of the Empire." Their mere physical presence was proof that the Raj was firmly intact and, more important, was reproducing another generation of colonial rulers. We have outgrown those days of Empire in many ways. But even in the twenty-first century, some people still seem to believe that perfectly behaved children should be trotted out as accessories. I know it's hard to put children and family first, but I believe parents should seriously consider making that choice in the first six months after the family's arrival in a new place.

Parents must be willing, at the outset, to make certain sacrifices when raising children in a foreign country. What good is some fantastic overseas assignment if the family is going to pieces because the adaptation process has been mishandled? Culture shock doesn't disappear by divine right. It can go away without wounding family relationships, though, if people are willing to acknowledge its existence and work together to get through it.

Chapter 4

THE CHALLENGES OF PARENTING GLOBAL NOMADS

WHEN LILLY WAS six years old and a first grader, she began studying the piano. We were living in Taiwan at the time, and pianos were easy to rent in Taipei. Our timing was right in another way, too. Taipei American School, which our daughter was attending, had just reopened on a new and improved campus. The larger facility could hold not only an ever-expanding student population but could accommodate many after-school activities, including music lessons. This was very convenient for parents like me who hated driving in Taipei. There was, however, some walking involved.

To meet her piano teacher, Lilly would need to go from one end of the school to the other. This represented a formidable distance to a paranoid mother like me. Parts of the school still resembled a construction site. I chose to wait for Lilly outside her classroom so I could help her navigate the dusty halls, past the unfinished, empty class-rooms. In reality, the only threatening obstacles along the way were older students racing down the hall to catch the school bus. Nonetheless, walking her to her lesson made me feel better.

Halfway through the year, Lilly decided she didn't need to hold her mother's hand anymore. She was old enough, she informed me clearly, to go from point A to point B without a guard dog. My first reaction was the response of mothers everywhere whose first-born child has just told them to push off: *Absolutely not!* Middle school kidnappers could be waiting to drag a little girl into all that sawdust. Maybe a dragon or two was lurking.

Rodney couldn't believe I was afraid to let our daughter walk such a short distance in the benign atmosphere of a school. (This was the same father who, a year later, would blithely put his entire family at risk on a flying park bench passing as a chairlift, at a mountain tourist spot in China.) He told me that the fears were in my head, and not about any school bogeyman scooping up our daughter and her piano books. I told him to go back to studying his Chinese characters and leave the after-school activities to me.

Although I knew Rodney was right, accepting what he'd said was another matter. I wanted my daughter to experience her first bit of separation from me, but I was unable to let go just yet. I came up with a compromise of which Lilly remained blissfully unaware until she was eighteen and we were reminiscing about our days in Taipei. She could go the distance by herself, I told my six-year-old daughter. Indeed, I told her how proud she made me. But on the day of her first lesson alone, and on each one thereafter, I hid behind every pillar and post between her classroom and the piano studio to watch over her, looking like the proverbial fumbling spy wearing a planter on my head.

TRANSFERRING YOUR OWN FEARS AND WORRIES

There isn't a parent alive who can control the simple act of a child taking her first steps toward independence. Nor can we prevent the terrifying events played over and over on television newscasts. But we can take charge of the way we deal with these stressful situations and of the way we come across to our children. When parents begin transferring their fears and anxieties onto their children, the fallout can be considerable. Children follow the parental lead on everything. If Mom appears afraid, that emotion will be transferred to them in a heartbeat. This is why parents must try to keep *their* fears hidden from their children—whether those fears are about terrorism, avian flu pandemics, or something as ordinary as a child going off on a school field trip to another country.

There can be little doubt that global terrorism and health crises like SARS have added a layer of stress for parents raising children abroad. The tension can be particularly acute in countries where there have been random bombings, destabilizing the world in the macro view and the expat family in the micro. "I think kids are scared," a Jakarta-based mother told me soon after the Bali bombing in Indonesia. "Children don't have adult powers of information gathering and sifting, so they are less able to manage their anxieties. Their imaginations are so fertile."

"The difference the kids see in their lives now, as opposed to before the terrorism began, is the reaction of the adults around them," a mother based in Kuwait posted in a message on my moveable families chat group after the attack in Indonesia. This sentiment is further reinforced by clinical social worker and expat author Carol Schubeck, who wrote the book *Let's Move Together*.

"Even young children can sense when there is a change in parents or care providers. They take their reactions from their environment, whether it's the school, teachers, parents, or friends," says Schubeck, who works with military families.

Schubeck offers concrete advice for expats parenting in stressful times, including limiting the time spent watching the news to once a day; monitoring comments made in front of children; educating children regarding the facts; discussing world issues with other adults when teens or children are not present; evaluating a school's crisis plan, and providing reassurance to children with daily hugs, pats on the back, compliments, and kisses, as opposed to material things. "Children need to be reassured that, while these are uncertain times and history is actually being made, you, as the parent, are there to protect them, just the same as always. Even if you are unsure of the future, remember that, to your child, you are their security blanket."

And while random acts of terror are part of the big scary picture, don't forget to keep an eye on the smaller stuff, too. A school field trip provides a good example, for international schools offer numerous opportunities for children to travel for sports, music, or culture. Sometimes a parent isn't comfortable sending a child off alone on one of these excursions (or the child herself may be hesitating). One mother living in Shanghai grappled with this problem. "When my daughter was in grade six, she was invited to participate for the first time in a model United Nations convention for middle schools in Guangzhou. There were no other girls from our school attending, except for another sixth grader and her older brother.

Schools have different approaches to these situations; some have a policy of only sending kids in pairs to host families, but this is not always possible. Some schools are also strict about the children staying with families, as part of the objective of the trip. This was a difficult decision for both of us. My daughter nearly declined the invitation because she felt uncomfortable staying in a home with strangers on her own. But with the support of a very understanding teacher she ended up going and had a great time."

This mother supplemented the teacher's support with a strategy of her own. "The teacher recognized that the primary objective was for the kids to participate in the UN program, not the 'homestay' experience," she said. "He also deferred to my judgment, saying that he was not a parent himself, that I know my daughter and knew what was going to be best for her. In the end, I traveled to Guangzhou separately from the school group and stayed in a hotel near the school, so my daughter knew that I was nearby if she needed me, and that at any time she could choose to come and stay with me at the hotel. Having this option was the safety net she needed to step outside her comfort zone and stay with a host family on her own. Without that, she may have missed out on a great experience."

Sometimes your solutions may not be the greatest, but if they work for you, who cares? It isn't a contest. Longtime readers of mine know that I'm an anxious flyer. I knew the chances of my fear of flying being picked up by my children were high, unless I could manage to look relaxed at all times—especially during takeoff, when I can be at my worst. I'm not especially proud of how I coped with this situation, which was to hide a cocktail of vodka and orange juice in one of my children's special juice cups. I would refer to this as "Mommy's juice," and I'd consume it in one big gulp as the plane went wheels up. It worked, though, and my children were never afraid to fly because of me.

By the way, your children may be hiding *their* fears, too. When author Dave Pollock first introduced me to the notion of "pre-traumatic stress syndrome"—worrying about something that *might* happen—he told me a story with a sad twist on this condition.

During one of his lecture tours, Pollock met a child who couldn't stop crying because he was so fearful over what could go wrong in his new surroundings. He asked the child if he had told his parents about his worries, and the child replied with a resounding *no.* He didn't want to scare his mother, he said, and worse, he worried he would ruin his father's career if he said anything. Pollock's interpretation, based on his lifetime of experience with global nomads, was that it had been ingrained in this boy that to voice his fears or concerns to his parents would be to let them down. It's very important, as parents, to give your children the opportunity to express their fears so they don't remain hidden and fester.

PLACING HIGHER EXPECTATIONS ON GLOBAL NOMADS

With their veneer of maturity, global nomads are too often expected by their parents to reach for a very high level of achievement. Like all children, they want to please their parents. Stop and consider, however, whether you might be placing the bar of your expectations for your kids frustratingly out of reach. We may be misguided in some instances by offering enrichment to our children.

Rodney and I learned that in a situation I believe other parents will find instructive.

At age fifteen, our son, Jay, was still so short that his friends towered over him like the giant fir trees of British Columbia. To distract him from worrying about whether he would ever grow, I decided Jay needed to build up his self-confidence. We arranged for him to go off during the summer holiday to Mexico by himself—ostensibly to study Spanish, but really to live with a Mexican family for a few weeks and make a journey on his own to a place where we had never lived as a family.

From friends and family members alike, all I heard was *Are you crazy!?* As a reader, you must be wondering how I could go from being the anxious mother hiding from my daughter to the woman loading my son onto a flight bound for Mexico City—with a change of terminals in Toronto, no less. But we had a connection in Mexico to a language school, and Jay would be living with a family accustomed to hosting North American kids.

About six weeks before his departure date, Jay confessed to me in the car on our way to school that he'd had a nightmare the night before in which he drowned. Being a regular teenager *and* a dream interpreter, he took this to mean his Mexico trip would end badly. I tried to calm both of us down by telling him, "Well, you don't have to go, you know. You have a choice."

He jumped all over that comment. "What choice do I *really* have, Mom? If I don't go, you and Dad will be disappointed in me. I don't want to let you down."

That stopped me dead in my tracks. Jay was right. Rodney and I did have high expectations that our son could do this trip on his own successfully. After all, he was no stranger to foreign places. At thirteen, he had gone off to Japan with his high school wrestling team—all eighteen-year-old *men*. I thought Jay could handle anything, but if he didn't believe it himself, we were being terribly unfair to him.

Before Jay got out of the car, I told him flat out that we'd been wrong to have assumed he could do this journey. And what's more, no decision was irrevocable. We would consider some new options over dinner that night, I said. That evening, we talked about these. Jay could go to Mexico with his father, who had decided he could take a week off work. Jay could go to Mexico just for a trip and check out the homestay the following summer. Or he could cancel the whole thing. Jay chose option A: he would go with his father.

The following morning, when I was again driving Jay to school for early-morning wrestling practice, I asked him if he had slept better. He assured me he had and then surprised me by saying, so quietly I didn't hear him at first: "I think I can go alone."

Say what? "You and Dad seem confident that I can do it," he said, "so let's stick to the original plan." My jaw dropped. Anxious to learn from this experience, I asked Jay if he had changed his mind because we'd admitted we'd made a mistake or because we'd rectified matters by offering him real choices. He answered yes to both points.

So that summer, Jay went off to Mexico. Rodney and I learned not only that constructive consultation is important, but that we needed to temper our expectations. Jay never complained again about being short. But it should go without saying that I didn't sleep very well the entire time he was gone.

A GLOBAL NOMAD'S CHILDHOOD WILL BE DIFFERENT FROM YOUR OWN

When I was Jay's age, going off to summer camp in another Canadian province was the extent of the enrichment and travel I was offered. If my father had ever come up with the idea of a Mexican adventure for me, I would have been sure *he* was dreaming. In my childhood, during the baby boom years, parents simply didn't know what was going on in their children's lives the way parents do nowadays. We would leave home on a Saturday morning (after the cartoons were finished on television, of course) and not come home again until dinner. Soccer was an impromptu game played on the street. And while I'm certain my father knew the name of my high school, my teachers' names would have been a blur to him, because he spoke to them once a year at most, during parent-teacher conferences.

Modern expatriate parents are not only over-involved in their children's lives (a matter I explore in the next section), but they also represent a unique niche demographic—the vast majority are overachieving type A personalities. In international communities, most parents are on the lookout for enrichment opportunities to serve their children's future. Whether it's a field trip to Greece or house-building in Cambodia, the cost of enrichment is more affordable for families living on overseas allowances than for those struggling to make mortgage payments at home. Expat enclaves may also be nothing like the communities in which many of us grew up, which had fewer financial resources but also a wide variety of personalities among their members—winners, losers, late bloomers, underachievers, hoodlums, geeks, rich kids, poor kids, and so on. There are worse things in the world than a high-achieving future for our offspring being modeled by successful professionals, but the choices we've made in our own lives—and want for our children, given their global upbringings—may not be the choices best suited to their personalities.

And how can a friendly neighbourhood where everyone knows your name and remembers you in diapers possibly occur in these global, mobile times? We live in a world that has seen more change in the past twenty years than at any time in history. Picket fences have all but disappeared, and chatty neighbours are usually busy talking to someone on their computers or their cell phones, not out in their gardens.

So, not only does that childhood of your past no longer exist, it's certain you won't find it in a foreign country. This is something you must accept from the get-go: your children's upbringing will be very different from yours. And your kids may well make very different life choices than you expect. Global nomads will grow up as internationally aware people, but not all of them will want to be mobile. We as parents need to respect that.

THE PROBLEM OF HELICOPTER PARENTING

Not heard this expression before? It means you're *hovering* over your kids too much, disabling them from taking off on a life of their own. It's a term applied to parents who are overmanaging, overscheduling, and generally overprotecting their children. The practice has become so prevalent now that some parents of university-aged students are calling up professors to interview them, or to complain about their children's grades, or even to find out if their son or daughter has been attending class. This is probably quite contrary to your own experience in childhood.

"Out of the goodness of their hearts, some parents treat their child as if she were a delicate crystal goblet," writes the American pediatrician, author, and educational consultant Mel Levine in *Ready or Not, Here Life Comes.* "Consequently, the child is shielded from adversity of every sort. This kind of perceived fragility has spread throughout our culture and is actually making kids fragile."

Some expat parents are aware they may be overdoing the worry. A mother based in Latin America wrote this message to my chat group: "I've started to worry that I may be over-worrying about my eldest son. He is eight years old, lived in three countries and has been told to learn to speak three languages so far. Now in grade three, he is struggling with friendship and organization in the class. So almost daily I've been checking his progress in class and the playground. I worry that he is alone in a new school. He isn't, but I still am concerned."

That mother herself is far from the exception. According to Dr. Levine, school principals are seeing so much parental intervention that opportunities for children to learn how to resolve their own disputes are becoming scarce. Universities now have orientations *for the parents.* Stop to think for a minute about what that means. Did *your* parents need to know their way around your campus? Dr. Levine wisely advises parents to remain on the sidelines, serving as sounding boards and offering advice only when needed. "Settling differences for a kid is one way to put him on a pedestal, possibly making him feel smugly invulnerable. Someday he'll experience the shocking realization that some disputes won't go away unless he actively negotiates settlements."

Dr. Levine isn't writing about expatriate children in particular, but he could be, from what I've observed in my travels and interviews. Children are being coddled and protected in many communities, to a degree that could threaten their ability later in life to form healthy relationships and gain proper job skills (a theme I explore further in the final chapter of this book).

When an expat mother tells me with a straight face (and so many have) that she is always connected to her children via cell phones for safety reasons, I want to ask what, not who, is being kept safe. Is it the mother's constant presence in her children's lives that is being saved? Some parents are phoned by their children dozens of times a day. Does this help them or *you?* Safety concerns aside (and, of course, those considerations are real and paramount), a child's confidence and ability to make decisions on her own are hindered if her mother can be reached at all times. And whatever happened to expat kids jumping on a local bus and seeing where it might take them?

Some parents keep an eye on things unobtrusively by volunteering at their children's school. "It allows a parent to observe the interactions children have with each other and with teachers, and to get a feel for the general atmosphere of the school as well as presenting the opportunity to know your child's classmates," reports one mother based in Antwerp. "It's not seen as interfering or checking up on the child or the school. There is so much that you learn by being in the school as a volunteer, and if there comes a time when you need to address an issue, you come to the table with a more informed understanding of what goes on, and hopefully a comfortable level of interacting with teachers in an everyday way. Teachers also have more respect for parents and their opinions when they have received your support in practical ways, and see that you are interested and committed to supporting your child's education."

Of course, children's free time is limited these days because of the new child zeitgeist of nonstop activities. On this note, more wise words of caution from Dr. Levine: "Parents who seem obsessed with delivering nonstop happiness for their kids may end up with children who, thanks to overindulgence, feel limitlessly entitled. Their feelings ultimately may lead to a sense of invulnerability, a belief that they will always get whatever they want without any effort or self-sacrifice."

Finally, let's not forget the endless supply of "stuff" to be bought while abroad now that global marketing has led former developing countries into consumer frenzy. An expat mom accosted me at a talk I was giving at a school in Southeast Asia and told me I should start speaking about *ex-brats,* as she called them—spoiled expat kids who do nothing but shop all the time, and still want more. I might have taken her suggestion more seriously if there hadn't been two giant shopping bags at her feet.

AND SPEAKING OF MONEY...

This might be a good place to raise the subject of money, specifically how to talk about the value of money with expat children. Like their parents, expat kids may see the local currency, at least at first, as "funny money." And for many expatriate families (though certainly not all), money is more plentiful abroad due to overseas allowances and other perks.

Opinions are mixed on the idea of giving children an allowance, but I tend to favour the idea; an allowance provides kids with the opportunity to learn about budgeting, saving, and the importance of giving some of their money away to charity. When children manage their own money and are given a finite sum like a clothing allowance (which we provided for both our children beginning at the age of fourteen), they also begin to be creative about earning it. Sometimes parents can help in this regard.

"When we were living in the U.K., my son had to earn money for a monthlong expedition to Namibia," one mother told me. "Since he was too young to work legally, and living in a culture where part-time work for students doesn't exist, I suggested he start a car-washing business on our street. He built up sufficient clientele to raise £3,000 for his trip over the period of a year and a half. It was hard work, but he enjoyed watching his bank balance grow, and it allowed him to develop a sense of accomplishment."

Good financial role modeling by parents is also extremely helpful. At the very least, stop once in a while to think about what kind of messages about money you are sending to your children. Don't live at the local mall or engage in a frenzy of impulse shopping, then chastise your children for doing the same.

OUTSOURCING PARENTING

From overparenting to ignoring the children: in expat communities you see both ends of the spectrum. When I meet parents overseas, I always stress that they must never leave the job of parenting to others. I'm emphatic on this point, especially to those living in countries where household help is available to do everything from laundry to cooking to babysitting. I've had that luxury, so I know how easy it would have been to let everyone else do my job while I played socialite and rode around in a chauffeur-driven car. I chose to do neither.

You can be a constant presence in your children's lives instead of outsourcing your job to tutors, coaches, and personal trainers. These days, though, many parents don't want to be the bad guy by saying no to a child. It's much easier to have someone else say it. According to Dr. Mel Levine, many mothers and fathers are downright fearful of their own children, especially teenagers. "Adolescents often hold the power in a family because they have so many weapons at their disposal (such as drugs, alcohol, tattoos, anorexia, suicidal thoughts, dropping out)… This fear may in part stem from a feeling of guilt that both parents are working and worry they are not devoting sufficient attention to their children." In the expat world, there may also be the guilt of transplanting a teenager.

In the overseas context, however, the job of parenting merely becomes magnified. Your children *especially* need you to say *no* now as much as *yes*.

YOUR UNHAPPINESS WILL AFFECT YOUR CHILDREN

Relocation experts are quick to point out to companies that an unhappy spouse has the ability to derail an assignment. That's why a growth industry of career counselors, work permit consultants, life coaches, and others has sprung up to help the spouse adjust to life abroad. A spouse's reluctance to relocate is still the biggest deal breaker in relocation.

But despite company support, an empathetic husband, and a legion of household help, some women will never be happy abroad. There can be many reasons for this: having to abandon her own career, finding that her husband is never around, fearing the new culture, hating the intrusion in her life of household help. Whatever the reason, the bottom line is that if the mother is unhappy, she has the ability to make her children unhappy, too.

Unquestionably, a mother's culture shock will lead to some very bad days. There may be tears, meltdowns, and a lot of screaming: mother at child, mother at father, mother at brick wall. But this does not make a woman a bad mother. It means she's human. Despite her hysteria, her children can (and do) survive and thrive. I have my own two children as evidence of this.

I'm not proud of myself for the way I would sometimes dump my troubles onto my poor daughter; Lilly told me long after the fact that she wasn't sure what she would find when she came home from school: a mother baking a cake or one lying comatose with depression on the sofa. My point, though, is that we got through it, and you will, too. Some days you'll need to cut yourself some slack. Usually, common sense should serve you well. But if your unhappiness gets out of control, you will want to seek appropriate remedies. Therapist Lois Bushong writes in chapter 8 about the signs indicating you may need professional help. Some Employee Assistance Programs and other company initiatives may be of use.

YOUR MOVEABLE MARRIAGE AND YOUR CHILDREN

Two key points need to be stressed to parents of all stripes and nationalities. The first is that your children are watching. The second is that nobody's perfect.

As I said in my book *A Moveable Marriage*, children need parental stability to feel secure about their lives. Yet consistency and balance in the parents' relationship may be two elements sorely lacking during and following a move. The needs of mobile parents are often sidelined in favour of the children's.

Among other things, adults require some peace and quiet after a major relocation. That's not going to happen with a fussy toddler or moody teenager in the house. But when kids see Mommy and Daddy being tense with one another, whether over dinner or over the phone, it's not ideal. It's especially not ideal for a child who has been moved thousands of miles away from familiar surroundings. The last thing you want your kids worrying about is a divorce. However, putting on a false front for the kids at all times isn't desirable either. You and your husband are allowed to be human. It's the amount of sniping at each other that becomes the issue. Try to keep things under control for the sake of both your marriage and the children. And know this, too: kids aren't stupid. They will use the perceived situation of marital discord to manipulate your guilt to their advantage and seize the moment: for example, to ask for a high-tech toy they've been coveting.

If your relationship does indeed start unraveling while you're abroad, you will probably want to seek counseling. Therapist Lois Bushong offers advice in chapter 8 on how to determine when your relationship has entered the danger zone.

DUAL-CAREER MARRIAGES

A forest's worth of trees has already died for all the literature published about the dual-career challenges of the mobile family. But let's knock down one more so that I can address the issue here, in the context of raising children on the move globally.

I have advocated with companies for years for employment opportunities for the accompanying spouse; I have written policies, I have advised and consulted, I have become sick of my own voice on this subject. And I have also played devil's advocate with married women who relentlessly pursue career opportunities abroad without considering the impact that may have on their global nomads.

Most women raising daughters want them to see us as fulfilled women, making our own choices and not bowing to media or peer pressure to choose between being a stay-at-home mom or a woman with a Big Career. It may be very 1990s these days to refer to the myth of Superwoman—who can hold down a meaningful, well-paid job while devoting the rest of her waking hours to her children—but in talking to expat women, I believe some things never change. The Mommy Wars still rage at home and abroad. In other words, women are still struggling to be all things to all people. That carries a price, and nowhere can that price be higher than for the family overseas, where, as I stress again and again, your children need you more.

I'm not here to argue the merits of dual-career marriages versus one-breadwinner marriages. (Read my book *A Moveable Marriage* for that discussion.) I'm writing this book to discuss the care and nurturing of your children, and I would be less than honest if I didn't say that mothers who go to work immediately upon arrival (and I don't mean the mother whose job brought the family abroad) place their families in as much risk as do their partners who are working 24/7.

I think, though, that a compromise can be reached: women can consider working part time and in the process shed the often debilitating notion that their identity is defined by what they do, not who they are. They may be reluctant to admit it officially, but I've chatted in my travels with many women working full time who feel stretched, stressed, and disconnected from their kids. Children need one front-line parent abroad. It can be either a father or a mother. But children do best when someone is keeping a close eye on the ball and is not too exhausted to *play* ball as well.

Having thrown in my opinion, I will acknowledge that dual-career marriages abroad are more and more common these days. If you are among the couples engaged in them, keep your eyes wide open for the impact your careers are having on your children. That means organizing family time and family trips as often as possible and designating one of you to be available for the inevitable emergency. And remember, the challenges you face in juggling careers made more intense in the expat context will always filter down to your children.

MULTICULTURAL MARRIAGES

When a multicultural marriage moves from one parent's culture to the other, there are bound to be tugs and pulls on the children. Parents raising bicultural children in this situation would do well to get the advice of experts who've gone before them down this rocky road. It's not a situation one should step into lightly, and gathering information and advice ahead of time can really help.

An excellent book on this subject is *Intercultural Marriage: Promises and Pitfalls*, by Dugan Romano. Romano addresses the subject of raising children abroad (although not necessarily global nomads) and makes this one particularly interesting point for parents: "Parents who clash over child-rearing issues are often really battling over some basic difference in philosophy, values, or beliefs that they as a couple have not managed to resolve; the child merely provides the spark for the conflict. But these underlying issues are often difficult to recognize or define, let alone come to grips with; so, instead of going to the heart of the matter, the couple fights over the particulars." Reading Romano's book will give you some assistance in avoiding this and other pitfalls.

THE SINGLE EXPAT PARENT

There are two kinds of single parents: the "single parent without dating privileges" I've described myself as being, because my husband travels so much, and the *true* single parent, going it alone in an international setting.

It would seem that *no* trees have died on account of the latter, for so many single expat parents have written to me over the years and asked me to address the subject. Single parenting is difficult at the best of times, but abroad it can be even more challenging, especially as the demographics of expat societies are, as Bridget Jones might have put it, *smug marrieds.*

If you are accepting an overseas assignment as a single parent, make sure that some household help is part of the bargain. You will also want to make every effort to build a support system for yourself on arrival. Parenting abroad is always stressful, and being a single parent adds a significant factor to the mix.

IF A DIVORCE OCCURS WHILE ABROAD

Marriages do break down abroad. I've seen it happen, with infidelity too often the reason, and I've found some women and men positively inspirational in how they handled themselves with such grace under pressure. There also are practical matters to be considered immediately.

I devote an entire chapter of *A Moveable Marriage* to marriages that go wrong abroad. I can't cover all of the same ground here, but one absolute must for the spouse of a man posted overseas is to find out exactly what you and the children are entitled to financially in the event of an assignment ending due to divorce (or worse, death) and to investigate how the sponsoring organization or business will handle either of those scenarios. As it's often the case, in a divorce, that the employee continues to work for the company and does not leave the post, some companies provide counseling for the mother (or father) and children upon their return home. But I have to state this plainly, given the anecdotal evidence that indicates high numbers of marriage breakups abroad: hope for the best, but plan for the worst. I've recommended many times, for instance, that couples should not sell off their family home before a posting abroad. If they do, it will mean there is no family residence to return to if the marriage disintegrates.

Most important to the subject at hand: try not to

involve the children in your battles, hard as that may be. Complicated visitation and custody rights may have to be worked out, so be sure to get everything in writing.

COMMUNICATING WITH YOUR GLOBAL NOMADS

If you get nothing else from this chapter, I hope I have made it clear that parents are only human. Your adult issues are naturally going to affect your kids in many ways, big or small. But there remain some key messages that you, as parents, are responsible for getting across to your global nomads.

• *Encourage feelings of gratitude.*
If your child isn't constantly reminded that not everyone gets to live and travel and do all the cool things your children are privileged to be doing, that child will grow up to be an adult with an inappropriate sense of entitlement. Remind your children often (especially if you are living in a poverty-stricken country) that most of the world is not living the way you are. Make family trips that are socially responsible to reinforce your kids' feelings of perspective and gratitude. And try to keep your own perspective. It may be fun to suddenly feel elevated to high society abroad, but parents with their feet solidly on the ground will have more success at keeping their children's feet there, too.

• *Refuse to tolerate bad behaviour.*
When our family was in transition, Rodney and I always let our kids get away with murder for the first few weeks. After that, it was "Let's get on with it now." But there should always be zero tolerance for rude, insensitive

behaviour toward other children and especially toward people working as household help. There are consequences for bad behaviour and these are known as discipline. Establish boundaries and limits, and stick to them. Consistency is the ticket.

If children learn from an early age that every success story is preceded by a few failures, they'll be better able to approach their own lives in this way. It's something you may also need to remind yourself of from time to time. Life doesn't always go smoothly; it isn't always fair, but we can learn from our mistakes when things go wrong.

Parenting can be a hundred times more complicated in a foreign environment, where everyday issues are magnified. Give yourself credit for doing it. The challenges of moving are to ensure that your family continues to enjoy each other's company, to support each other, to become active members of your new community, and to seek out and appreciate all that life abroad has to offer.

Chapter 5

RESTORING WORK-LIFE HARMONY IN EXPAT FAMILIES

RETURNING HOME to Vancouver once from an overseas speaking trip, waiting in a slow-moving line at the airport's passport control, I envied my master-of-the-universe road-warrior husband. When he disembarks, Rodney passes quickly through a "cornea control" line. Eyes bloodshot from a twelve-hour flight may cause a momentary glitch in the machines, but Rodney doesn't face nearly the delays foisted on us ordinary mortals.

We had missed seeing each other a week earlier: Rodney's flight to Vancouver from Korea, the last stop in another of his lunatic five-countries-in-ten-days itineraries, had landed just minutes before mine took off, bound for Shanghai. I knew from his calls and e-mails that his trip had exhausted and depressed him. He had become sick with a particularly vicious cold, and the antibiotics given to him by a hotel doctor somewhere in India had only worsened his condition. Still, he had plodded on.

"I have no choice. I *can't* come home yet. I'm the president," he had whimpered to me over the phone. I reminded him of the punch line to our running gag: "Remember, I'm not coming to Mumbai to collect your body." He was too sick to laugh at his own worst nightmare.

When the doors of the arrivals hall finally flung open for me, I was grateful to spot Rodney. He waved, but he seemed to be watching the crowd with a strange intensity.

"What are you staring at?" I asked.

"At me," he replied enigmatically, then explained.

Bursting through the doors as if a starter's pistol had gone off, pasty-looking, dehydrated road warriors had sped past him while he waited for me. They tightly gripped the handles on their carry-on roller suitcases, garment bags and computer bags slung over their shoulders. With their free hands, they plastered cell phones to their ears, placing calls to colleagues or clients. They'd probably already sent several e-mails via their BlackBerry since their planes had landed. The only eye contact they made was with the signs pointing to the exits.

"I'm one of those guys," my husband confessed sadly. "It's demoralizing to watch."

"You're not one of those guys," I reassured him. "You *always* call your mother when you land somewhere." Actually, I could picture him looking as self-important as those road warriors. But my comment brought a bit of colour into his face. Besides, I reap all his air mile rewards, so I definitely wasn't going to kick my gift horse in the mouth.

MANY MEN BALANCE WORK AND LIFE WELL

Readers of my books or those who have attended my lectures are aware that I use Rodney as a convenient whipping boy. He's never there to throw in his two cents' worth or give his side of a situation I'm moaning about—

whether it's his extended business travel or a household emergency like a water heater exploding when he's far away.

Well, I now come to praise him, and the many other men who successfully juggle the demands of working globally with the needs of their spouses and children. Throughout this chapter, I will be referring to an Internet survey I conducted to gauge how men balance work-expat life challenges. While some are in complete denial (they have no problems, they say, although their marriages have ended, they've had a heart attack or two, and their children are strangers), most claim to be having the time of their lives working abroad. Contrast that with the expat wives who responded with answers like this one: "My husband travels every week, and I am at home with four children, coping with teenagers and school exams. My poor husband tries to fix everything in two days, and we all end up arguing."

Since I was often left at home to cope with two children, a nutty dog, a snowstorm or two, and the regular household emergencies, I could easily relate. But Rodney has done an amazing number of things right. (Okay, I made a few suggestions.) We're still happily married after more than twenty-five years, and despite his being absent from our home for probably a third of that time, he has a very close relationship with our children.

How did he do it? More precisely, how did we as a family manage to maintain peace and harmony in our household given the demands of his work? In this chapter, I want to share our successes as well as to offer suggestions from other families who have achieved that balance. But first, a little background.

WORK-LIFE BALANCE IS THE WORKPLACE ISSUE
OF THE TWENTY-FIRST CENTURY

Many factors contribute to work-life balance going off the rails, but topping the list is the modern-day on-demand life, in which everyone is expected to be reachable and there's no time to engage in something simple like sharing an evening meal with family or friends.

"Work-life is not just about finding 'physical time.' It's about the 'cognitive space' necessary to process, organize and respond to the thinking demands of life within a complex society," write researchers at Georgetown University in Washington, D.C. Apply that concept to a global context and we're off and running. The last bastion of peace and quiet—the long flight home, on which a business traveler could unwind, sleep, and quietly process a trip—has now been shattered by the introduction of in-flight Internet access. The boss can e-mail an employee in the air and expect a reply. Worse to come is the possibility of a cell *yeller* in the seat beside you, if the gods are truly crazy and allow the use of cell phones at thirty-five thousand feet. Air rage will climb to an entirely new altitude unless either common sense prevails or mobile phone users are seated, as they should be, on the wings of the plane. Clearly, a new phase of work-life stress is just taking off.

As I've said, in expatriate life, the regular day-to-day challenges are magnified. But nowhere is the *interdependence* of work, life, and family more enhanced than it is for expatriate families.

The issue first surfaced domestically when more women began entering the workforce in the 1970s. In the case of women with children, it became obvious very quickly that it was exhausting juggling child care and a full workload, and that wasn't even counting the second shift at home. So, men were needed more at home to pick up the slack, and many have done just that. As a woman's earning power has increased, so too has her power (in some cases, anyway) to insist that her husband help out more on the domestic front.

The expatriate world, however, is still very tradition-al. The vast majority of expatriate employees are men, and they are typically the sole breadwinners. The often reluctant stay-at-home wife is stuck back at the new house due to an inability to gain a work permit in the host country or a career that was nontransferable.

How many times has an accompanying spouse and mother, desperate to have more of her husband at home, been told: "We're here because of my job. And if that means I have to work fourteen hours a day and travel half of the month, that's just the way it is!" The wife simply has no power to insist otherwise. Or, as an expatriate spouse wrote in response to my Internet survey: "What spouse? Oh yes, the guy that travels from country to country, and sometimes manages to be home for the weekend!"

The balance of power in traditional expatriate mar-riages resembles a 1950s scenario—man as sole bread-winner, woman at home looking after the domestic front—and this is the reality many expat families face. But it's still possible to achieve a better work-life balance while living and working overseas. In the following pages, I'll present some ideas on how to do that.

FATHER'S WORK-LIFE IMBALANCE CAN DERAIL THE FAMILY

Balancing the needs of the job and the family is important in general, but it becomes even more crucial in the international world of work. Many global nomads rarely see their fathers. The father's constant absence from the family unit—even when he's not away, he's online or on the phone—can be *the* top stress for a family living abroad.

When I speak to business audiences about the needs of the expat family, my main talking point is this: an unhappy spouse can make or break the international assignment. But I want to take a slightly different tack here by emphasizing that a stressed-out husband and father, trying to keep both home and office happy, has the ability to derail the family.

Companies find it easy to shuffle the issue of work-life balance for their global employees to the bottom of the heap. As with dual-career challenges, they treat it as a "soft" issue despite the fact that it can deliver a hard wallop to the bottom line, notably in lost productivity while an employee puts out fires at home. But I don't want to focus here on organizational denial of the issue. Nor, indeed, on the increased competition of the global marketplace, which is often cited as the reason for work-life imbalance. "Anybody who refers to 'global economic forces' as a rationale for abandoning work-life balance is speaking from a policy, not a personal perspective," writes Susan Cramm, a former corporate executive and now a coach on executive leadership. "Work-life balance isn't about having more free time. It's about devoting your life and the hours within it, [in a way] consistent with your values and passions. Work-life balance is personal." In other words, it's an individual's responsibility.

As a speaker, when I look out at the numerous parent audiences I'm privileged to address, I see many fathers. They are passionate about their children, and they often ask questions. I know they want to make changes that will contribute to a happier childhood for their offspring. They just need some help.

Susan Cramm says it best: "If your values extend beyond yourself and your boundaries extend beyond the four walls of your company, you must face the uncomfortable reality that the solutions to work-life balance must come from within." So, allow me to help fathers "see" themselves for a moment. It's only when they step back and dispassionately view how they are behaving (in the same way my husband did with those road warriors at the airport) that they can begin to take the necessary steps toward change.

WHAT MAKES AN EMPLOYEE RUN SO HARD?

Rodney's insistence that he couldn't cut short his trip that time, despite his ill health, had baffled me. Surely his physical condition should have been his primary concern. What on earth was going through his mind when he chose to remain on the job instead of taking to a sickbed?

For some answers, I turned to a very enlightening book. In *For Women Only: What You Need to Know about the Inner Lives of Men*, American journalist Shaunti Feldhahn surveyed four hundred men, between the ages of 21 and 75. The author stresses that her study wasn't searching for an understanding of men's *outward* behaviour (like working through a bad cold) but was addressing "the inner thought and emotions that led to their behaviour."

For instance, did men honestly want to be working their brains out?

"What they really want to do," Feldhahn says her survey revealed, "is park on the recliner and command the remote. But in reality, for most men, the need to provide is so deeply rooted that almost nothing can relieve their sense of duty." Even single men feel this way, the author concluded when one unmarried respondent explained that "if he didn't provide for himself, other people would have to, and he would no longer be in control."

Control is about power, of course, and men feel powerful when they are good providers. This, however, is a "desirable goal as well as a burden." An intense burden, too, Feldhahn hastens to add. As another respondent put it: "Maybe you should see this as the flip side to how we think about sex. About sex, men are pretty utilitarian and women are emotional. About money, work, or providing, women are utilitarian but men get emotional!"

A comment from another of Feldhahn's respondents was also telling. This one was given in response to a woman concerned about her husband working too hard: "Why do you think I *do* work this much? It's because I care about you!" This man had been traveling for his work for almost twenty-five years, and his wife had never understood that, from *his* point of view, he was making a sacrifice—out of love and a desire to provide for her.

Obviously not all men can lay claim to that excuse. Like journalists craving the *bang bang* of a war zone, some men relish the adrenaline rush and the near-psychic addiction to living on the edge, which in this case means working all the time and, not coincidentally, avoiding the day-to-day tedium of raising children. My own experiences with business travel, when my children were younger, were that it provided a welcome relief from diapers and the chance to order up a room-service supper in a hotel room. Those lazy evenings on the road had vanished by the mid-1990s, when e-mail needed to be answered at the end of a long day and the cherished club sandwich eaten in haste. But I still enjoy being on the road (once the flying is over) and being responsible for no one but myself. It's like I have permission to be selfish.

Shaunti Feldhahn suggests that women should try to appreciate a mate's drive to work, provide, and succeed *as long as there is some balance* (my italics) and the home relationships stay strong. A man can feel caught by the need to keep an employer happy with his performance and provide his family with a paycheck that allows them to buy the material trappings a consumer-driven society tells us we want.

Feldhahn's is not just one of the thousands of "chick" books that explain how to keep men happy. The same point was made in the *Harvard Business Review on Work and Life Balance*. In that collection of papers, sociologist and feminist Michael Kimmel, in a contribution entitled "What Do Men Want?" writes that being a provider lies at the core of a man's identity. "[After all], a man's profession and his ability to bring home a paycheck have traditionally defined who that man was."

It can make no difference at all if a man's wife earns enough money or even more money than he does. It's his job to earn a living for his family, and he can't switch off that gender imperative for a moment. That would be akin to turning off his identity.

Professor Kimmel does, however, add that the role of

men has undergone a transformation since the 1990s: "A new organization man has emerged, one who wants to be an involved father with no loss of income, prestige and corporate support—and no diminished sense of his manhood. Like working women, we want it all. Yet in today's insecure corporate world, we're even less sure of how to get it."

Author and journalist Gail Sheehey, who has been charting the changing passages in the lives of both men and women for over thirty years, confirms in *Understanding Men's Passages* that the values many men grew up with have been subverted. Furthermore, she notes the game between employers and employees has also changed. "Now the corporation is a virtual father—amorphous, nonhierarchical—and you can never be clear where you stand," writes Sheehey. "[A man's] whole identity is tied up with the status he has achieved so far. If he lets go, even a little, what else is there?"

BUSINESS HAS A STAKE IN THIS ISSUE

Margaret Shaffer of the University of Wisconsin, a management professor and highly respected academic researcher on expatriation and repatriation, believes it's critical for business reasons that organizations develop a better understanding of how expatriate employees deal with the increasingly heavy demands of both work and family. "Within the organizational domain, a balanced relationship between employer and employee leads to better performance," Shaffer argues in a 2001 academic paper published in the *Journal of Management*. Her reasoning is multifaceted, but she quotes oft-cited statistics to prove that, without organizational support—needed much more by an employee who has relocated, often with his family, to a foreign country—an assignment may be doomed from the beginning. If logistical support is not offered, especially when there is an expectation it will be forthcoming, Shaffer believes this leads to the employee's "psychological withdrawal" from the job, which can cause an early repatriation. Furthermore, Shaffer says, a "crucible for stress" can be created as an expatriate employee struggles for balance between work and family.

Shaffer's logic is in step with human capital theory, which in layperson's terms argues that employees can become dysfunctional when they face excessive demands from either home or the office without the necessary support. That same theory also suggests that an employee's personal resources can run out. In other words, people can only hold it together for so long.

"These resources are *time* (allocated to behaviors) and *energy* (both physical and psychological)," writes Shaffer. "People prioritize broad domains of activity (e.g., work, family and leisure) that they are willing to allocate to resources and then make choices about how to spend their resources. Time and energy are exhaustible commodities. Once spent, they are not available for other tasks."

Global employees can easily get trapped in that time and energy crunch, especially if they are working through multiple time zones. The "globalized day" truly does have twenty-four hours. Increasingly, organizations expect certain outcomes to be achieved during that extended time period. One particular response to my own survey appeared many times in only slightly altered form: "My husband is a workaholic, but working overseas is much more strenuous, with longer hours than back home. He works during the day, but at night, when it's morning in the West, he is expected to be in video conferences."

Yet when an employee asks his company for support (in the global context, this can mean relocation assistance for the family, for example), he is too often told the organization provides enough financial rewards already or simply can't afford to offer any ground support.

My Internet survey confirmed what is common knowledge anecdotally: long working hours are creating disengaged, exhausted, and, in some cases, burnt-out employees. "My husband works for a company that is closing a U.S. plant and opening one in another country with many new products," wrote one respondent. "He works twelve to fourteen hours a day in a high-stress environment. He has little energy left for his family."

"My husband's company and his position demand that he put in long hours and time away from home," wrote another spouse. "Meetings are just called and he is expected to attend, even if we have already bought tickets to something or the children have a school event. It's a feeling of being owned. Our entire way of life is being held hostage in someone else's hands. My husband chooses work events over family and school events most of the time. He feels obligated to be available for work."

Shaffer's research on work-family balance focuses primarily on the employee's psychological withdrawal from work. Clearly, what still needs to be tackled in the academic literature is the way work causes the employee to psychologically withdraw from the *family*. Again, there is much anecdotal evidence to support the following response to my survey, an oft-repeated sentiment:

"The single biggest issue affecting me as a relatively happy long-term expat is the time factor—with a partner having a lot of responsibility and a lot less time to spend with the family. There is no family life left!"

Business may have been listening with half an ear, and keeping a close eye on the bottom line, when it came up with the "short-term assignment" as a way of not having to uproot a family to fulfill a company's global commitments. This scenario may be well and good when the family stays in the "home country" and puts up a master schedule to keep track of when the "master" will be home. But often, it is families already transplanted abroad who are put under further stress when the working partner is sent away on a short-term assignment. That expression, by the way, is an elastic one; the term can be as short as a few weeks or long enough to break the family's patience. Likewise, there can be stress on the family when extended business travel in the region takes the father away from home Monday to Friday. The "single parent without dating privileges" scenario I mentioned earlier comes into play here. Families go along with these arrangements, having little power to make any changes or ask for more support.

WHEN THE ROAD WARRIOR COMES HOME

Who doesn't know (or is married to) the guy who comes home exhausted after a marathon day or a business trip too tired to do much of anything? Like most men, he probably also doesn't want to talk about it. Of course, he has legitimate reasons. He wants to get away from his work. But refusing to speak about it, brooding, or looking like hell only alienates and worries his wife more. She may not be in top form either, if she's been left alone for days or weeks to cope with the children. And needless to say, this guy is not engaged with his children.

Like many women, this wife may insist and prod (as I've done with my own husband), forcing her partner to finally open up. So he shares his problems, and then, seeing the distressed look on her face, he responds (and rightly so) with "But you wanted to know how I felt!"

"Connecting emotionally may also feel strange and even frightening to a man who has been taught to associate manliness with being a fierce, solitary competitor," writes Gail Sheehey. A man who doesn't want to share may work longer hours because it's easier than talking to his wife or bringing his problems home. The kids are upset because Mom, who can't exert control over anything except them, is driving everyone nuts. Everyone is miserable.

And according to Margaret Shaffer, the more committed an employee is to his work, the less time and energy he'll have available to spend with his family. And so the catch-22 grows, because the harder an employee is working, the more reliant he will become on family or on recreational or community time to recharge. As Shaffer notes: "The only domain from which one can draw the needed resources is the domain that is generating the conflict in the first place." Throwing money at the problem, a knee-jerk corporate solution, doesn't work either, because it's not money that's the source of the stress. (Although most men will tell you money is *always* the problem.)

An expat employee who finds himself in this position may feel his only choices are to leave an assignment prematurely, take early retirement, or leave his marriage. For those who do stick it out, with marital and family strife and unpleasantness at home, the stress of the situation can lead to serious physical and mental health issues. The company's bottom line is negatively affected by the employee's ineffectiveness on the job. The employee's personal well-being and the health of his marriage and relationship with his children hang in the balance. And he's dead tired from trying to juggle it all.

Many successful executives keep on going, according to Michael Kimmel's report in the *Harvard Business Review*, by putting their problems in boxes. But even the men he refers to, who compartmentalize this issue in order to label themselves as good fathers, good providers, and good men, all "reported stress and irritability; half had trouble sleeping; most had few close friends."

CROSS-CULTURAL WORK-LIFE CHALLENGES

Let me throw one more issue into this mix: the cross-cultural challenges associated with work-life balance in an international market. A manager assigned for the first time to an Asian country with a very strong work ethic, for example, goes into deep corporate culture shock when he discovers that not only does his home country expect him to work a thousand hours a day, but the local culture insists upon it. Drinking after hours may be considered part of the job, too. Alternatively, the guy may *want* to get home early, and may even be working in a country whose culture supports the importance of home and family. Head office culture, however, certainly doesn't.

One new mother who responded to my Internet survey reported on what her husband faced at his office. "The locals excitedly asked my husband if he had rearranged his schedule to take time off each week to be with our new baby," she wrote, citing the required flexibility toward a shorter work week for employees in the country of their assignment. "My husband looked at them as if they had two heads. He didn't feel he could explain that to his [third-country] board of directors who assigned him at great expense. He thought they would think he was slacking off. As it is, he travels for his company and works almost twelve hours a day on most days."

A second respondent to my survey told me about another cultural factor at work. "The employee often feels pressured (or grabs the chance) to become more macho when a family moves from North America or Europe, for instance, to a society which has a different idea about equality. This further upsets the fragile balance of power in the marriage, which shifts in a former dual income family when there is suddenly only one breadwinner and the other party becomes totally dependent on so many levels."

THE ROAD TO BURNOUT

All roads for the employee, regardless of where they begin, may eventually lead to burnout. And that's not good news for the family unit.

"Burnout is the gradual process by which a person—in response to prolonged stress and physical, mental and emotional strain—detaches from work and other meaningful relationships," according to *Mental Health Month*, an Internet-based newsletter. "It can result in lowered productivity, cynicism and confusion. A person at this stage feels he is drained, exhausted and has nothing left to give."

In our overstimulated, demanding world, burnout is very real, and it's not a condition to be shrugged off. "In addition to feeling anger, cynicism and helplessness, burned out managers—those who expend a great deal of effort without visible results—often suffer from physical symptoms such as headaches, chronic fatigue and an inability to shake colds," writes Harry Levinson in his award-winning essay "When Executives Burn Out," published in the *Harvard Business Review on Work and Life Balance.*

According to Levinson's research, burnout manifests itself in various ways and to different degrees, but it appears to have highly identifiable characteristics: chronic fatigue due to sleeping problems; anger at those making demands; self-criticism for putting up with the demands; cynicism, negativity, and irritability; a sense of being besieged; and hair-trigger displays of emotion. "When people who feel an intense need to achieve don't reach their goals, they can become hostile to themselves and to others. They also tend to channel that hostility into more defined work tasks than before, limiting their efforts," reports Levinson. "If at times like these they do not increase their involvement in family matters, they are likely to approach burnout."

Unfortunately, becoming more engaged in family matters is not something that can be turned on and off like a light switch. Emotions are involved, too. "My husband's biggest challenge with work-life balance, I think, is guilt," wrote one woman, echoing the opinion of other respondents to my Internet survey. "He is very aware that he has uprooted all of us, so it better be worth it! That is a pressure that I think can interfere with day-to-day work and life."

Therapist Lois Bushong points out that burnout and depression often go together: "An interesting difference between men and women in this area is that when women get depressed, they withdraw by sleeping or pulling the drapes shut. When men get depressed, they get angry. But they can't afford to get angry at their employer as they would lose their job. So who gets it? The spouse or family."

Ultimately, Bushong points out, a man may choose to avoid the fighting at home by spending more time on the road. This leads to further burnout and depression, especially when he comes home and dumps his anger onto his family. The cycle, she warns, can become a vicious one, lasting until the man crashes and burns.

Factor in the threat of obsolescence facing the aging baby boomer worker; a lack of control over workload, schedule, and deadlines; the absence of feedback, which makes an employee feel unappreciated; petty conflicts among workers or between workers and management, and anxiety about job security, and you will find a burned-out man or woman. Worse, for many it becomes the norm.

"I think my partner does experience work-life imbalance," a respondent wrote, "but after such a long time we have become accustomed to the long workdays and weekends. But isn't it sad to find this becoming accepted and the norm rather than the abnormal? I sometimes think we have lost sight of a 'normal' life."

Burnout doesn't happen overnight, though. It builds slowly, until suddenly he goes down in flames, taking the family down with him. And here's the good news: that doesn't need to happen.

STRATEGIES FOR REGAINING BALANCE

Want to reduce the possibility of burnout and increase quality time as a family? There are many strategies that the individual employee and the family as a group can devise to alleviate spiraling stresses. Gain control of your life by taking action, rather than sitting back and being the author of your own demise, is my first piece of advice for the expat employee. Since I suspect this will be the chapter a wife bookmarks for her husband to read, I'm going to speak directly to men here with my suggestions. (But ladies, read through to the end, as I have a few words for you, too.)

- *Get over yourself!*

Whether you're a road warrior or a workaholic employee or both, you are *not* indispensable. Ego drives too many employees into a mindset that makes them believe the world will somehow collapse without them. It isn't true.

Any guy who heads for the beach during a vacation specifically taken to relieve the stress of his job, then wraps his computer, BlackBerry, and cell phone in a beach towel, must *know* he looks like an idiot. Beach toys are allowed on holiday, but not high-tech toys. Clinging to them is foolish, not only because your wife and children are likely to be furious with you, but because you're buying into a dangerous cycle that can only lead to tears: your family's, for certain, and your own (withheld, of course) tears of frustration, mixed in with bitterness and resentment at the company that expects your vacation to be just an extension of the working day.

Who cares that the office claims they need to be in touch? Chances are they didn't mean 24/7, and it is *you* who feels so important that you are unable to disconnect. Why did they give you the time off for a holiday if they planned to have you work through your windsurfing lesson? A really good manager wants an employee in good health, not one who returns from holiday more wound up than before he left. So turn off the machines. It's the only way to turn off the head that goes with them. The world of work will survive without you for a week or two. What are you scared of? That your company might actually agree? Or that you will lose a job that is killing you?

- *"Switch and link."*
In the research for their book *Just Enough: Tools for Creating Success in Your Work and Life,* authors Laura Nash and Howard Stevenson learned from surveying hundreds of employees that successful professionals find ways to "switch and link" the focus of their full attention with lightning speed among activities that provide feelings of happiness, significance, achievement, and legacy.

In an interview in *Fast Company* magazine, Nash reported that too many employees are looking for a magic bullet or the one-stop solution. Moreover, she believes that the concept of balance itself is misleading. Using "switch and link" as a tool means taking a break to celebrate with staff over winning a contract—or, more important to this discussion, leaving your cell phone behind when you're on vacation.

- *Stand up to a bullying manager.*
We've all met the manager who brags he's always in touch with the office, probably responding to e-mail during the birth of his second child. If you work for a guy like that,

be sure you take what is owed to you from time to time—
a well-earned rest.

You can leave the office, be there for your family, and
not ruin your career. Countless successful people have
done it before, and countless more will do it in the future.
They are smart enough to know when enough is enough.
This personal wisdom probably contributes more to their
business success than anything else. They don't rely on
flashing high-tech business totems to proclaim that they
are someone important. Stand up to that bullying manager rather than skipping an important milestone in your
child's life. You'll be happy in later years to remember
your attendance at that high school graduation, first performance in a play at school, or final game of a baseball
season. Refuse to work on yet another file that is going to
mean missing something important in your family's life.
I am reluctant to raise the flag of the 9/11 disaster, but
after that horrific event, the media kept reporting that, as
they saw their deaths coming, people were calling *home.*
They were not calling head office somewhere else to say
"Sorry, can't finish the file."

• *Get regular exercise and use common sense.*
One executive I interviewed, who had turned down a
promotion because it would have interrupted his kids'
high school experience, shared some other lessons he had
learned along the way. "To better manage my travel I
started to force some discipline and common sense into
my travel schedule. A short break every three months
helped, as did lazy weekends. For years, I have kept a work
schedule that gets me into the office fairly early and
always back home for supper with the family when I'm in

town. Going to the gym at lunchtime is difficult, but a great way to reduce stress and force a break into the day.

"Get the family fully sorted out before you focus on the job," this man advises the relocated expat. And while living overseas, invite family and friends to visit so that they can share your experience. "Plan long weekends and vacations in order to fully exploit family time together as well as seeing the sites and experiencing your host country."

Proactively managing work-life balance is critical, according to this smart fellow: "If you wait for a tragedy to occur, it will likely be too late to fix it."

The commonsense part of this advice also pertains to your behaviour on the airplane. I've been lucky at times to fly at the "front of the bus" and observe road warriors closely (or been forced to listen to so many of their problems that I've been tempted to interrupt their monologues with *I think you've mistaken me for your wife*), and I can now quite definitively place them into two categories: healthy and walking heart attack. The latter is the guy who begins with several cocktails and every proffered before-dinner snack; he orders both red and white wine to accompany his mains and later hits the port or brandy with cheese. Then, when by all reasonable expectations he should be passed out cold, he fires up his computer instead of getting some rest.

• *Take time to make friends.*
If you still know anyone who is not a business colleague or contact, go see that person. Laugh a bit and have some fun. Look up from your spreadsheet. A computer offers no companionship and rarely has a sense of humour. One woman who responded to my Internet survey wrote

about an excellent idea her women's club came up with: "We created a men's interest group for the first Thursday of every month, at the neighborhood pub. I suggested it because my husband needs friends. Several of the men actually do show up and hopefully feel connected to something outside of work."

Another way for a busy man to make friends is by volunteering as a coach of a child's athletic team.

• *Be home at suppertime.*

Early in my own marriage, I laid down a "home for supper when you're in town" rule. Remembering family supper hour from my own childhood, when we all broke bread together and shared the news of the day, I knew it was a tradition worth preserving. Traveling was a fact of Rodney's working life, but if he was not away on business, I expected the children to see his face at the dinner table.

When our daughter was about twenty or so, Rodney thanked me for imposing that rule. It taught him to work more efficiently, and he is now very close to his children. Try it. It works.

• *Give your family time to adjust when you return from a trip.*

When you come home from a business trip, don't feel you have to immediately reintegrate yourself into the family, and into your spouse's good books, by rearranging the cutlery drawer in the kitchen. I can't count how many women have told me that that particular action (is there a cutlery fetish that has gone unreported?) was the straw that broke their own exhausted backs. Resist the urge to take over when you return, too, as this can make matters worse. Respect the discipline and rules your wife has laid down in your absence.

"When he is away, I am responsible for all the decisions with our life here," an expat wife wrote in response to my survey. "This includes what the children can and can't do. I become the bad parent when Dad comes home and lets them get away with things because he feels guilty that he is away so much or he is tired and wants to avoid confrontations."

Consider instead the advice I offer in *A Moveable Marriage*: institute the twenty-four-hour holding rule. That means everyone goes to their respective corners for twenty-four hours and makes no demands on each other. (If you're only home for twelve hours between trips, make this the four or six-hour rule.) I came up with this particular gem after some extensive travel by my husband prompted me to ask him if he only came home for clean shirts and sex.

Rodney and I also took up golf, despite it being the most frustrating game on the planet, because there's no room for confrontational conversation on a golf course. You and your wife will always be on either side of the fairway looking for lost balls.

• *Learn to listen.*
I've heard this scenario so many times: a woman spills her guts to her husband, who immediately starts offering solutions she didn't ask for. She just wanted a sympathetic ear. So learn to listen. (Women: this works *both ways*. If you want your husband to open up and share his stress—so that you can find solutions together for restoring balance in the home—listen dispassionately when

that's appropriate. Discussion can follow when the time is right.)

• *Stay in touch while you're away.*
The greatest advantage of e-mail is the ability for the traveling employee to stay in touch with his spouse and children through different time zones. The dreaded phone call home from the road, which always seems to come at the worst time for the spouse, can be supplemented by e-mail, text messages, digital photos, and all those other technology gadgets many of us haven't yet figured out how to use.

Still, there's nothing as good as a phone chat between father and child, as this wonderful story from a respondent to my survey—who describes her husband as a hands-on father despite all his responsibilities—shows: "Our second child had a bad day at school [while my husband was away]. He called home to check in and spent several minutes talking to her on the telephone. I had it on speaker, and I could hear how patient and tender he was being, trying to give her advice. Her tears turned to giggling when he told her to picture the girl who'd been bothering her with her underwear twisted if she was mean the next day.

"This was just one example of him putting forth the effort to work on the balance between family and work," this woman continued. "He was in Switzerland traveling from one meeting to another, but he helped me by helping our daughter. Instead of working while traveling, he called home because I had sent an e-mail to his BlackBerry. I was at my wit's end. He was aware of the situation and called to help out."

Note: if you're worried about a lengthy phone call to the family turning up on the company expense account, invest in "Skype" technology or any of the other free Internet service provider solutions that allow you to speak with your children over the Internet.

• *A word for the women: Do with less "bling."*
I can't say how many women have complained to me about their husband's long working days or extended absences from home while flashing fingers weighted down with bling (that would be diamond rings, for we regular folk who don't wear them) and wrists swollen with gold bracelets. His working less will mean that *you,* the spouse, might also have to make do with less (less handcrafted furniture; fewer five-star holidays; less shopping, period). This will also be true for your children. On reflection, surely that's a reasonable price to pay.

Much of the research being done now on work-life balance puts the emphasis on "enrichment" rather than on the ephemeral notion of balance. I like to use the word "harmony," as it sounds both gentle and attainable. Taking the steps to restore harmony in your home should be your number one priority. Your family is worth it.

Chapter 6

LEARNING ABOUT SCHOOLS

OUR DAUGHTER, LILLY, was entering grade six when we moved from Canada to South Korea, a country where children compete in the classroom as if every pop quiz is an Olympic event and only a gold medal is acceptable.

Rodney and I were old Asia hands by that time, so you'd think we would have had some inkling about the impact of Asian values—in particular the reverence for education—on the school system. Lesson number one for the newcomer to overseas schools is this: the values of the local culture definitely influence even so-called international schools. In South Korea, for example, as throughout Asia, those values (as I joke with both affection and the utmost admiration) are pumped up on steroids.

When we repatriated to Canada from Seoul, Lilly was so far ahead in school she skipped the eighth grade. She's not the first global nomad this has happened to, either. (Conversely, coming from a school that is less rigorous, some students may be behind.) So my poor daughter, who was very petite for her age, spent several months at a new high school being identified as that strange short kid who had moved from Seoul and skipped a grade. Not exactly the handle she was aiming for.

PARENTS MUST DO THEIR HOMEWORK

Parents fret a lot about their children's education, yet I'm sad to say many put more time and effort into researching apartments, health clubs, or how to ship their cars overseas than into investigating the educational institution that will be the foundation of their child's new life. So it's important to stress that parents must do their homework and learn exactly what their children will be facing. It's crucial that you get this one right.

International schools come in several varieties. Some offer American or British curricula and are considered international because they are open to all English-speaking students. The growing popularity of International Primary Curriculum (IPC) has created another form of international school. Some countries have also set up their own national schools abroad, France, Germany, and Japan among them. There are even some Canadian schools. Depending on where you will be living, as I noted before, there may be a large local population holding U.S. passports; this allows children to attend so-called American schools, a term that may only mean the school has an American curriculum.

Numerous holders of other passports enroll in the English-speaking international schools, as these provide a wonderful opportunity for a high-quality education in English. The downside for non-Americans can be the primarily American content. My daughter learned about Abe Lincoln before she knew about Sir John A. Macdonald, the first prime minister of Canada. On a positive note, all of her teachers throughout our time abroad issued an open invitation to parents who wanted to introduce content related to a child's own culture.

The choices available for your child's school will depend entirely on the size of the international community. If you are headed for the new "hot posts" like Dubai, for instance, there will be multiple schools to choose from; in other locales, there may be only one. Parents need to learn quickly what kind of demand there is for spots in these schools, as waiting lists are common. The last thing you want, if you are moving with two or more children, is to find out there is not enough space to allow your children to attend the same school. Schools will often advise parents to place their child in one school while waiting for a place to open up at another. I recommend against this; it may mean separating your children, and even if it doesn't, once your child feels comfortable at a school, you won't want to move him again. By the way, it's funny how siblings who hated each other at home can become best pals abroad. In fact, one of the first things I taught my own two children when they were old enough to understand the idea was the importance of growing closer. When it came to memories of childhood, they would always have each other.

PARENTS' INTERACTION WITH THE SCHOOLS

Expat parents need to establish a healthy and friendly relationship with international school administrations, especially those parents moving in midyear or moving north or south of the equator into a different school year timetable. I've met families who were advised to place a child at an inappropriate level, one that was either too advanced or too slow. You can be so overwhelmed when you first move somewhere that you defer to the school too easily. But remember, no one knows your children better than you do, and you must act as their advocate. You can be a well-mannered advocate (that approach is recommended over being pushy and rude), but if you feel your child is not being placed at the proper school level, you must say so.

Likewise, if your child has any special learning needs, it's imperative that you discover *before* leaving home whether the international school will have the resources to address a learning disability or a language deficiency. Many employees who accept a job abroad don't admit the entire truth about the needs of their children until it is too late. International schools have traditionally catered to the status quo, although they are employing more counselors and special education teachers as children's needs are changing. As a parent, do not leap before you look. It will be your child who takes the fall.

Many international schools, through their hard-working parent groups (which I suggest you join or support at the earliest possible moment), provide transition and culture shock adjustment training that the schools—and teachers—would otherwise ignore. Some schools, such as the American School in The Hague, have set up school-wide transition programs involving parents, teachers, and students. However, many international schools are almost as bad as multinational corporations when it comes to recognizing the emotional needs of children and budgeting to accommodate training programs. Fair enough: the schools are there to teach math, not about culture shock. But I find it slightly humorous when I speak at international schools (at talks typically organized by the school's parent organization) to find so few teachers in the audience. Teachers want to do right by their students, and I believe they would do well to realize that there's more to teaching global nomads than achieving a perfect score on a math test. It's ironic, since many of them have their own global nomads with them, but sometimes teachers need to be reminded that they once had culture shock, too.

INTERNATIONAL SCHOOL CULTURE SHOCK

The biggest culture shock of an international school, as one American father put it so succinctly to me years ago in Taipei, was the shock to his bank account. International schools do not come cheap, and this can be a blow to your financial system if the school fees are not covered by your company or organization. Do try to negotiate those fees as part of your overseas package.

If the school your child will be attending has a high percentage of the local population as students, expat parents must also be prepared for cultural considerations to enter the classroom. And it won't just be the local culture that's driving the school bus. One of the most positive characteristics of international schools is the diversity of their student populations. But if your children are transferring from schools where there has been very little diversity, this will be a shock to them. It may also be a shock to parents when they meet the mothers and fathers of their children's classmates. "Getting involved in the parent association means being willing to be part of a multicultural team and not expecting to do it all the American way," notes Barbara Schaetti.

Even international preschools and nursery schools will reflect the expat community's cultural diversity. One American mother of preschoolers wrote to me about her experience in South Korea: "The Europeans expect nursery school to be a big play date and are shocked and offended when the local (Korean-run but English-speaking) preschools here actually have learning associated with them. And we Americans assume there will be teaching done at the preschool level. On the other hand, the Europeans have no problem sending their tiny toddlers off to nursery school, whereas the American moms look at using the toddler programs as shirking the duties of the stay-at-home mom. I find this area rife with strong cultural biases, depending on where you come from."

Depending on the school, it may also be a shock to your children when they receive their first report cards. If they are entering an overachieving school, they may not do as well as they did at home (where they also weren't distracted by having just been transplanted into a foreign country). Self-esteem and self-confidence may drop with their grade point averages. Many international schools also place a much higher premium on grades than on sports, which will be a major shift for children coming from some Western cultures. Conversely, if the new school your children attend is below the standard of your home country or of previous postings, your kids may become bored or coast along unchallenged, since they have already covered the material. As parents, you need to keep a close eye on things to ensure your children receive a balanced education.

MOVING TEENAGERS INTO NEW SCHOOLS

Although school challenges exist at each age and stage of childhood, moving teenagers into a new high school presents the biggest challenge for expat parents. A change in school during a teenager's life, more so than for an elementary school child, does mean a profound upheaval, and it can be truly traumatic if not managed properly.

For teenagers, school is much more than a place to sit and study math or geography. It's the center of their social world. Teenagers typically form close relationships and bonds at school, and the friends they make there become crucial components of their lives. Fitting in is a vital part of a teen's existence. This helps explain why teenagers have a more intense reaction to news of an international relocation. Exacerbating the situation is that, developmentally, teenagers are undergoing significant physical and emotional changes at the same time they are learning to form their own values and make independent choices.

The choice to move is definitely out of a child's hands, as any expat parent knows well. In many instances, the employee and his or her spouse have no control over the relocation either. The result is that too often a teenager's needs get short shrift. Parents may be overwhelmed by the logistics of a move. Companies or organizations offer little, if any, predeparture preparation for teens, and many international schools, as I mentioned, are only just learning about the benefits of "transition" programming for global nomads.

Elizabeth Perelstein, president of School Choice International, has identified some factors that can help parents evaluate how easily their child, particularly if a teenager, will adapt to a school in a new country. For instance, she recommends asking these questions: What kind of student has the child been? In what educational circumstances has he or she thrived or, conversely, struggled? What kind of person is the child socially? Does he or she make friends easily? Does the child have any interests that will transfer easily and facilitate new friendships? The answers to these questions will help parents evaluate a teenager's transition challenges in a new school environment.

Academic considerations vary from place to place. For children of any age, but particularly for a teenager, it's essential for parents to consider the curriculum that the child is leaving behind and try to coordinate it with the curriculum she is moving to.

Parents fretting about their children's education abroad need to know that they are not the only ones lying awake at night worrying. In her coaching practice with expat clients, Margie Warrell, an Australian expat spouse with four children, confirms that one of the most difficult choices parents face when deciding to go international or to remain abroad is where to educate their children: in local schools or international ones? the host country or in a boarding school in the home country? "I hear so many educational concerns from parents," reports Warrell. "Parents want to know where their children will best fit in socially and culturally but, also, which schools will provide them with the broadest educational and social experience. They also wonder if those schools will reflect their own social and educational values. And, naturally, they wonder how their child's educational experience will place them if they are moved again in another two years to a new country."

Despite a growing awareness of the unique needs of mobile children and teenagers, much more needs to be done to assist parents helping their children through difficult transitions. Even choices made with the best of intentions can turn sour. One expat family living in Mexico accepted a posting precisely for the cultural experience they felt it would give their teenage children. However, they ended up sending both a seventeen-year-old daughter and a twelve-year-old son back to the U.S. for their schooling. That wasn't a foolproof solution either.

"I'd love to say that things were perfect when my daughter arrived back in the U.S.," this mother told me, "but she had missed the first half of her senior year and missed out on many of the cherished senior moments. She wasn't in the high school yearbook, wasn't in the senior play or at the senior Christmas dance. She went home from Mexico changed, but there was hardly one change that was positive." Luckily, things did get better, this mother reported; her daughter is now her old self once again. "Her transition to college was painless: she's extremely independent, assertive and compassionate."

This family also struggled to find the right situation for their son. After pulling him out of a local Mexican school, his mother told me, they'd first tried the home schooling option, but that didn't suit her very sociable son. The family finally opted for a boarding school for him back in the U.S.

"There is no right time to move a child," says School Choice International's Elizabeth Perelstein, "nor a specific time at which a child becomes too old to relocate. Each age presents trade-offs. Sometimes the secondary years are the threshold that employees, who are parents, are unwilling to cross." But remember, she adds, that when they do move into international settings, teenagers regularly find peers who are accustomed to moving and faculty trained to accommodate varied curricular backgrounds.

"It's important that parents get very clear on the pros and cons of the different options they face in educating their teenage children," advises expat coach Warrell, "and this includes their choice to be an expat in the first place." She believes many parents haven't given the issues as much thought as they should beforehand and then find themselves overwhelmed by circumstances for which they aren't prepared. "I ask parents a lot of questions to really hone in on what it is they value for themselves, their children, and their family unit," Warrell says. And, once a choice is made—whether it be to go local or to send children off to a boarding school—she tries to guide parents to a state of reconciliation with their decision. "In the end, they have to make a choice and live with the consequences."

Elizabeth Perelstein offers some excellent ideas on what to ask for from your company or sponsoring organization by way of support for making educational decisions. These include checking to see whether the company posts a list of other parents who have had positive experiences with international schools, so you can contact them for information and reassurance; asking to meet with international school personnel on any look-see visits to a potential posting, and requesting funding for an educational counselor to walk you through this particularly stressful process. Ultimately, parents may need to redefine "education" itself, says Perelstein. "If education means more than classroom time and is broadened to include the cultural enrichment offered by an overseas assignment, then relocating a teenager will be well worth it in the end."

Not every expat family opts for the international school, especially if education has to be funded on their own nickel. Toddlers and preschoolers have an entirely different set of play groups, nursery schools, and kindergartens as options. (Some of these may also be expensive, though; find out in advance so you can ask the company or sponsoring organization to pay.) Home schooling, boarding schools, and local schools are options for school-age children that many parents select.

• *Play groups*

I don't know how newly arrived mothers with toddlers would survive without play groups. Think of these as baby study groups. Even if the children just stare at one another, the mothers find soul mates right away, and they learn where to find important baby items in the new location. Community centers, websites, local chat groups, even your locally hired caregiver will probably be able to point you in the direction of a play group near you. If all else fails, I suggest stopping another mother out with a stroller and introducing yourself.

• *Preschools and nursery schools*

Many of the references you will get for preschool options will come by word of mouth, but Western-style nursery schools based on the Montessori system and others are all to be found now in most highly populated expat communities. There are some standard areas of investigation you should undertake regarding preschools, such as the pupil to teacher ratio (the smaller the better); the availability and safety of facilities, and the look of the place (is the school painted brightly?). Is there a playground on site or nearby? What kind of equipment does it have? Have a good look at the school's toys to see what kind of selection there is. Will there be a bus ride to the school, and how long will it take? (When I shipped my poor son off to a nursery school in Beijing, a good one, he had to sit for half an hour on a school bus.) Finally, how many days a week can children attend the preschool, and how long are the sessions? If you take your child with you, you can size up a school in a few minutes by watching how she reacts to the environment—and, more importantly, how she is greeted by the school staff.

• *Home schooling*

Parents choose the home schooling option for personal as well as educational reasons. They may not be able to afford the international school in the new location, or they may not agree with the school's philosophy. Another common reason for choosing this option is the lack of resources in the school system for a child with special needs, whether that child has learning difficulties or is gifted. Regardless, home schooling is not a choice to be entered into lightly in the overseas context, and it requires parents do their research before making the decision.

One mother considering the option as a way of offering enrichment to her young son feels home schooling "might actually be one of those opportunities of a lifetime for a family who is struggling to make a school fit their child, or worse, to make their child fit the school.

For example, I see home schooling as giving me the ability to go with my child to those cultural activities which are too crowded to even consider on a weekend or a national holiday. Or to be able to immerse him more in the local experience than skim the surface as we busy expats with little ones tend to do."

Fortunately, for those who do choose home schooling, you'll have a new best friend in the Internet. The Web offers curriculum resources and distance learning, interactive programs, global and even local connectivity. One mother investigating the possibility for her gifted child found a large local group who had chosen this option and were providing support to one another.

• *Boarding schools*
Sometimes there is no choice but to send your children to a boarding school. There may be no high school available at your new posting, for example, or no school consistent with your cultural values. Parents who are offered a move in a teenager's final year of high school may choose a boarding school in the home country as a way to allow the child to stay put. (Remember, though, that going to boarding school still involves a move.) If it's possible for your child to remain at their school and board with another family, that might work if the details are handled properly. Once again, do your homework, not only on the school you choose but also on your child's ability to be on their own. Selecting a boarding school that is close to extended family members can help in avoiding lonely holiday weekends.

• *Local schools*

Many expats dream of taking their children abroad and dropping them into a local school. Not for these parents the giant international schools! The local option may be a good one if your child is already fluent in the local language or has a facility for learning a language quickly. Otherwise, you are dropping your child into a situation that may sound romantic but can be a nightmare. Think long and hard about this choice, and be sure to seek out the advice of other parents who have gone this route.

SCHOOL CHALLENGES FOR THE CROSS-CULTURAL CHILD

By cross-cultural child, I mean the child who looks like a local but isn't a native speaker. If his school is populated by locals, this child will face some identity challenges. A lot will depend on how the two parents' cultures come together in the new location. Many cross-cultural expat couples who return to the country of one partner find transition difficult. Many of the pressures to choose "who they are" can be transferred to their children. As parents, you'll want to do a lot of communicating in the early days to make your children feel grounded and secure, so that they can present themselves with confidence to their new classmates. Barbara Schaetti believes this can provide a great opportunity to help a child deal with complex issues of identity.

CHILDREN WITH LEARNING CHALLENGES

As noted earlier, special programs for students with learning challenges may not be on offer at your international school. You may need a consultant or other expert to help you find the right school for your child or, to prepare your child to live away from home if a boarding school becomes the only option.

THE ONLY CHILD

Like only children everywhere in the world, the global nomad without siblings may have undue attention placed on him at home and expect the same attention in the classroom. Without a sibling running interference for him in the days before a friend is made in the new location, it can also be harder to settle in. But only children have developed their own survival and coping skills. As parents, you'll need to rely on your child to find his way in a new school without interfering too much, despite the temptation.

THE CHILD WHO GOES OVERSEAS FOR THE FIRST TIME

Seasoned global nomads, while still resisting new family relocations, have developed skills over the years for integrating into a new environment. This is not the case for a child on their first overseas assignment. Luckily, in the international school system, there are so many new students at the start of any school year that, even if your child is an expat neophyte, she will quickly find someone else looking dazed and confused and join forces in friendship.

THE CHILD WHO ARRIVES MIDYEAR

I am asked often about the impact of moving a child in the middle of a school year. This scenario can happen in the context of domestic moves as well as international ones. Is there an adult alive without a childhood memory of a new classmate who arrived at school one day out of nowhere, looking as if they would like to vanish into the ether?

The challenge of fitting into a new school midyear is magnified in an international setting. For one thing, the academic standards of the new school may be different from those of the child's previous school. Throw in factors such as culture shock, the age of the child, and the relationship between the parents, and it's obvious a midyear move is not a decision to be entered into lightly. If you have any choice in the matter, try to move on the school schedule.

Finally, I want to stress again the importance of getting involved with your child's new school in an overseas setting. Not only will your child find this a positive sign of your interest in them, but your involvement in the school community is a wonderful way to help create a new "extended family" for celebrating holidays far from home, traveling within the country, or just getting together with other parents to compare notes on the weekend. If you stayed away from parent organizations before you moved abroad (and let other parents handle all the volunteer work that enhanced your child's life), now's your chance to repay that debt.

Chapter 7

KEEPING THE FAMILY HEALTHY

OF ALL THE ISSUES that consume expats and expats-to-be, matters of health are invariably close to the top of the list. Being sick is bad at the best of times, but when it happens in a foreign country, it can be downright unsettling. Given the worries about SARS or pandemics in recent years, there are good reasons to be prepared. Even with the best-laid plans emergencies will happen, and they always seem to happen first to your children. Just ask Lilly, who broke her arm a month after we moved to Beijing when she jumped off a chair. Naturally, Rodney and I were out for dinner and unreachable. Luckily, we came home to find that our embassy community had kicked into high gear for us.

Expat families need to be prepared for the unexpected. Preventive medicine is always a good practice, and it's important to learn what's available locally *before* you need to use the hospitals. As an expat parent, you must take personal responsibility for your family's continued good health. I hope the information in this chapter will assist you in that endeavour.

SETTLING IN

After a few days or weeks in your new location, the exhaustion and disorientation of jet lag will mercifully lift, leaving you as close to clear-headed in a new culture as you can reasonably expect to feel. Your stomach finally grumbles at the correct time of day for the appropriate meal. Everyone feels almost like themselves again. Children may be showing a spark of independence at last, exhibiting fewer of the intense emotional aftershocks (and crying jags) that may have appeared soon after arrival. The moving boxes may have arrived and been unpacked and your belongings put away. What now?

Before charging out the door to embrace your new life and all of the adventures it holds, you should put some time into the critical health issues still on the agenda. How best to go about finding practical health information in an unfamiliar country? The short answer is: ask a lot of questions. Begin your research by scouting out the local medical resources you may have found initially online.

FIRSTHAND INSPECTIONS

Nothing replaces a firsthand visit to a hospital or clinic or face-to-face meetings with physicians or hospital officials. These will help you make comprehensive decisions about your family's health care needs. Never turn down a tour being offered by a women's club, an international school, or your own embassy. When we lived in Beijing, I foolishly passed on a visit to a major local hospital the Canadian embassy had arranged. My rationale? It was still early days, and my adjustment to Beijing was tenuous. I figured a visit to the hospital might send me into an emotional tailspin and set me on the road to the airport.

When Lilly broke her arm, I didn't have a clue where the hospital was or any idea of what the inside looked like or (and this was critical) know that to get to the part of the hospital that catered to foreigners, you had to follow a special route down back lanes smothered in bicycle traffic. Sound confusing? It didn't need to be, if I had joined the tour when it was offered. When we were assigned to Seoul, I was first on the bus for the hospital tour.

In health matters, as in everything associated with expatriate life, you must be proactive. And if you ask nicely, your request will most likely be accommodated. If your local group doesn't offer a hospital tour, why not organize one? It can normally be arranged with a simple request to a hospital's administration or through one of the numerous joint-venture health services companies that have sprung up to help expats navigate the medical maze.

To maximize the benefits of any tour, it is useful to know what you are looking for. Here are a few guidelines to help.

1. Does the staff speak English?
Communicating a medical need can be difficult under normal circumstances, but it will be especially so if the language barrier is profound. Therefore, a question high on your list should be whether the hospital has any English-speaking staff. If so, is that service provided twenty-four hours a day? In other words, if you fall sick in the middle of the night, do you need to wait until morning to tell someone how you feel? If the service is not provided around the clock, designate a person who speaks

the local language who can be called upon to take you to the hospital in an emergency.

Another key point to investigate is whether there are English-speaking nurses on the wards. Although physicians often speak English, the nursing staff provide most of the care, and they are less often able to communicate other than with a smile and a pat on the shoulder. If English is not your first language, be sure to ask what other languages are spoken by hospital staff.

2. Is there an emergency room or an outpatient clinic?

The first is critical, the second ongoing. Go see both places, and count how many people are waiting to be helped. Are the waiting rooms clean? Are there bathrooms handy? Is the service handled in an orderly fashion or by the crush system? While you're at it, ask whether the hospital offers other specialty facilities, like an intensive care unit, a critical care unit, or a birthing room.

3. Is there a pharmacy on the premises?

Look around to see if there is a dispensary for prescription medications. This is important, especially if you will be seeing your doctor at the hospital's outpatient clinic. Life will be easier if you don't have to traipse to another part of town to get a prescription filled, and the medicines at the hospital pharmacy may be more reliable as well.

4. Is the hospital close to where you live?

Time how long it takes you to get to and from the closest local hospital. Do you need to fight your way through the most bottlenecked of intersections to get to it? When I was pregnant in Bangkok, I had a choice between an old-world colonial-style nursing home (which sounded wonderful) and a brand-new medical facility that happened to be ten minutes from my home by car. My obstetrician had privileges at both, but the nursing home was farther away from where he lived. I chose the facility closest to our apartment (yet still had nightmares of my doctor being held up in traffic while I went into labour in a cab).

5. How will you pay for services?
Will that be cash or VISA? Find out exactly how consultations and prescription medications can be paid for. Will the hospital or clinic bill you if you have a resident's card? It could happen that on a day you need medical attention you have no cash on hand, and there's no ATM handy. It's also worth asking whether there are two price rates, one for foreigners (typically higher) and one for locals.

It bears remembering too that when you are being discharged from hospital you should make sure your bill is carefully itemized. Unless you ask, in some developing countries your bill will only show a single charge for an operation. No insurance company back home will accept this, so you can save yourself an endless stream of correspondence by getting an itemized bill from the outset.

6. Can you see for yourself?
Will the hospital allow you to have a peek at the operating and recovery rooms? Move from there into a semi-private room (if one exists) and then a ward. While you're at it, ask about ambulance service, and if there's an ambulance parked outside, poke your head into that, too. Don't laugh at this suggestion: when we lived in Seoul, we found out that all those ambulances racing through the

streets were only conveyances. They had no paramedic equipment in them at the time.

7. Are there enough staff?

While you are busy roaming the halls, try to notice whether there's a lot of staff on hand. In some cases, the nursing staff may be so small that family members must personally attend to a patient. A close friend of mine had her appendix taken out the day after Christmas years ago in the Indonesian city of Bandung. She never closed her eyes unless there was a family member sitting quietly beside her, watching the IV drip into her arm.

HOW TO SIZE UP A NEW DOCTOR

Parents you've met in the playground or at school, or the local consulate, an international chamber of commerce, the school nurse, or even a hotel manager may recommend a doctor if your child gets sick. But remember that your idea of medical qualifications and the host country's idea may diverge. And "recommended" does not necessarily mean an endorsement.

Cultural differences may arise in the question-and-answer exercise I'm about to suggest. Some old-style doctors don't answer questions the way new doctors are now obliged to do or else risk depleting their patient rolls. If a new doctor seems unwilling to take the time to answer your concerns, strike their name from your list. A physician with the inability to provide satisfying answers—especially when you are living far from home and may be presented with diseases you have never even heard of before—is not a doctor you want to see on a regular basis or in whose hands you want to put your family's care.

If the doctor is willing to answer your questions, pursue your inquiry along the following lines:

1. Where is the office located and when is the physician available?

Is there parking? Can you get to this location easily? When we lived in Taipei and Lilly had a cough that just wouldn't dry up (it sounded like she smoked three packs a day), Rodney and I traveled to the locally recommended hospital half a dozen times over the period of a month. The hospital, which is where the pediatrician had to be seen, was without a doubt the most inconvenient place in Taipei at that time. Make sure your doctors are as conveniently located for you as possible.

Likewise, inquire about office hours. If someone else needs to drive you to the office (and that someone is only home after working hours), make sure to find a clinic or private practice that has nighttime hours as well as daytime. Ask about emergencies. Is the physician on call? Are they able to treat minor trauma? And here's a question for you: is a sterilizer for medical implements in plain sight?

For families living outside major city centers in areas where there are no clinics or hospitals, a good question for parents to discuss is what you will do in the event of an emergency. Bone up on medical evacuation protocols.

2. Ask about language, again.

Does the physician speak English, or do you share a third common language? Does the office staff speak English, so that if you phone in an emergency you aren't blocked by incomprehensible responses that make you even more frantic?

3. What are the doctor's affiliations?

You might think that hospital privileges are a matter of course for a doctor, but they are not. Ask your local physician where they have privileges, and follow up by checking at the hospital that these privileges do exist. At the same time, ask about access to labs, X-ray clinics, or other facilities required for tests. While you're at it, ask whether immunizations and vaccines will be available, and query their source.

4. Inquire about credentials.

Medical certificates are framed and placed on office walls to be inspected. Find out where the physician trained. Although a postgraduate degree from a well-known medical institution does not ensure quality care, it does let you know that the physician has been exposed to a wide range of medical care technology.

5. Throw in some personal questions.

Don't be afraid to ask the physician a few personal questions in order to determine biases. It is in doing this, for instance, that a doctor's resistance to answering questions may come to light. You might discover that issues requiring longer than a breezy ten-minute examination will not be a part of the service.

KEEPING A HEALTHY HOUSEHOLD

As you settle into a new home and a new routine, you can avoid trouble if you take steps right from the start to establish a healthy household. It never hurts to err on the side of being overzealous. Depending on where you are posted, here are some hygiene procedures you may want to consider establishing.

Keeping drinking water safe should be your number one priority. Water-related diseases are a major problem in some countries, putting both travelers and foreign residents at risk. Never be cavalier about your drinking water. When we lived in China, before the country's development took off, keeping the water in my home safe seemed to consume endless hours at first. However, once I got my routine down, the family could drink with some measure of confidence and I still had time for a life.

If local water is not potable, expatriates may discover that their companies will pay for bottled water. Remember, though, that bottled waters (especially those bottled locally) are not always safe, and the water in them should be tested and then boiled if necessary. You should definitely do this if you have babies. In places where water quality is dubious, avoid iced drinks and fruit juices that may have local tap water added.

Eating the local cuisine (and shopping in local markets) is part of the cultural experience, but it's wise to be careful about eating food sold by vendors. It may smell great while it's cooking, but the washing-up may leave something to be desired.

Are there Western-style supermarkets where you live? This doesn't necessarily guarantee safety, but if a store is the primary food source for expatriate residents, chances are it's been through a few inspections. Always check expiry dates, and never buy food in tins that have been damaged in any way. Milk may come fresh, but eggs can be another story. Are they refrigerated in the store? Or are they sitting on the shelf alongside the cereal? (The latter was the case when we lived in Beijing, prompting a good friend of mine to joke that if she ever wanted to kill herself, she'd use an egg.)

Local people hired to help keep your life on track are not mind readers. They need to be shown exactly how you wish to keep your household a hygienically safe place, especially those who will be working in the kitchen and buying food. As a first precaution, before you hire anyone, send them off to your physician (with the money to pay for it, if need be) for a physical examination. Chest X-rays and stool and blood samples are among the most important tests. If you have a baby or youngsters in the house who will be spending a lot of time with hired help, it's especially important that you be sure those people are in good health.

To keep the entire household in good health, lay down hygiene rules for everyone—especially your children—and enforce them as diligently as possible. With household staff, this will definitely include the washing of hands as well as the washing of fruit and vegetables. Make spot inspections of your kitchen from time to time to keep everyone on their toes. If you have the luxury of a cook, make sure that person doesn't smoke and cook at the same time. (I'm not making that one up.)

THE MOST COMMON AILMENTS

Even the best-laid hygiene strategies won't protect you against a virus, and even the most diligent people forget the rules once in a while. Although it's the highly infectious and humanly transmitted diseases like AIDS or SARS that take up most of the newspaper space, many expats moving abroad should worry more about the diseases popular in affluent countries. To put it bluntly, the odds are higher that an overweight, cholesterol-ridden, sedentary individual will have a heart attack than that he will contract encephalitis. But there are certain ailments you can fall prey to while you are adjusting to a new climate, new foods, and possibly higher levels of pollution than you ever thought possible. Here are a few to protect yourself from.

1. Pollution-related illness
The growth of industry in rapidly developing nations, and particularly the number of cars on the road, is causing extreme pollution in cities from Mexico City to Shanghai. This can mean immediate upper respiratory infections for the newcomer.

Depending on where you are coming from, your body will need time to adjust to the new irritants in the air. This can cause a phlegm buildup like none you have ever experienced, giving you the racking cough of a chain smoker. If you suffer from asthma, emphysema, or chronic bronchitis, you should do some research before you leave home, and you should think twice about taking an assignment in a city known for its pollution. Stay inside on days when the pollution is particularly bad. Humidifiers, dehumidifiers, and air filters can help reduce contaminants in your household. If your symptoms simply won't quit, you may have to consider moving.

2. Allergies
Along with pollution-related ailments come respiratory allergies. Spores, pollens, and other naturally growing materials can bring on allergic reactions. When we lived

in Taipei, Lilly developed an allergic cough that doctors referred to as "the cough white children get when they move to Taiwan." Although I blamed the Taiwanese capital for giving my daughter her cough, I might have been hasty. True enough, the pollution didn't help her case, but an allergist later confirmed that Lilly was prone to allergies and was going to develop them anyway. Taipei just pushed things along ahead of schedule.

Food allergies may induce uncomfortable rashes and worse. Since moving or traveling through an unfamiliar country means new, unfamiliar foods, people prone to food allergies should be ever vigilant and not eat blindly off a plate without first checking the ingredients. You can test certain foods by starting slowly (as one does with a baby, teaspoon by teaspoon) to see if you will have a reaction.

Allergies are another of those gray areas in which expatriates have to take personal responsibility for their health. If yours are severe, you should probably stay away from highly polluted cities.

3. Viruses

If there is a virus floating out there with your name on it, you are going to get it, regardless of how diligent you are about hygiene. Most respiratory viruses will respond to symptomatic treatment with antibiotics; however, the difference in strains may make expats more susceptible, especially at the beginning of their stay. When we lived in China, the first winter "Beijing flu" felled all of our family. (Finally, we got the original, not a Western knockoff.) Medical people nodded sagely and informed us this was "first winter in China" syndrome. And they were right. The second winter, when our immunities to fight off viruses had been built up, we sailed through winter without major bouts of flu. Staying fit and in general good health are also good defenses against illness.

For neophytes considering antibiotics for treatment: these have no effect on illnesses caused by most cold and flu viruses. They can even be harmful, for they may eventually render an antibiotic useless against a particularly bad super bug. For antibiotics to be helpful in treatment, their use must be properly regulated. Sadly, this is not the case in many countries. Be warned also that antibiotics can bring on yeast infections in women. If you must take antibiotics for a long stretch, ask at the outset for medicine to combat the inevitable yeast infection.

4. Gastrointestinal illnesses

Delhi Belly, Bangkok Belly, or Montezuma's Revenge: the cramping, diarrhea, bloody stools, and flatulence that accompany a gastrointestinal ailment don't need a name to be placed high on the list of undesirable and debilitating illnesses that can befall the traveler or expatriate.

These illnesses are typically caused by bacteria or parasites present in food or water. The most common bacteria causing gastrointestinal problems is salmonella. Symptomatic relief includes sticking to a clear fluid diet, then adding rice and bananas and, when required, over-the-counter remedies such as Imodium or Lomotil. If any gastrointestinal problem worsens after two to three days, seek out medical help from an approved physician.

CHILDREN CAN BE AT SPECIAL RISK

Common ailments often pose special risks for children. For instance, when children fall sick with gastrointestinal troubles, there is increased risk from dehydration and electrolyte imbalance. Be sure to keep a young child drinking clear fluids and add, if possible, salt or some electrolyte crystals to their juice. If a readymade preparation like Gatorade or another sports drink that contains electrolytes is not handy, here's a home recipe that is equally effective: mix together 1/4 teaspoon of salt, 1 teaspoon of sugar, 1 cup of boiled water (8 ounces), and add a bit of lemon juice for flavour.

Children also have a nasty habit of wiping their noses and then rubbing their eyes, which can cause conjunctivitis. Other eye infections can be contracted in swimming pools in tropical countries, and eye and ear infections may also be caused by pollution. Any of these infections should be checked out immediately by a qualified physician.

Children are exposed to more potential illnesses in their classrooms and through household help with whom they may spend time. The local environment may be more threatening to kids, and they are more likely than adults to forget the dangers inherent in eating an unclean piece of fruit or drinking something with ice in it.

The best advice for keeping your children well is to drill them on the rules and drill them often, whether those rules concern avoiding water fountains, keeping their hands off unfamiliar animals to avoid rabies, or not touching strange-looking flowers or plants that are pretty but could be poisonous. And while you are reminding your children about the rules of good health, remind yourself.

EXPANDING THE FAMILY OVERSEAS

Conventional wisdom says there is no good time to have a baby, but I beg to differ. If you are living in a foreign country, can't work, are ready to start your family, and are fortunate enough to have first-class, affordable help available, it should be full steam ahead, in my view. This opinion got me into serious trouble with some angry feminists in the U.S. in the early 1990s when my first book, *Culture Shock! A Wife's Guide*, came out. It was considered so politically incorrect of me to cheekily suggest women should consider having their babies abroad that major U.S. bookstores would not stock the book. But I'm sticking to my guns on this all these years later. Women who have never moved abroad because of their husband's jobs (and that would include the feminists who told me I was setting women's issues back twenty years by making expat women appear "dependent") know absolutely zip on this subject. For many expatriate wives, having a baby overseas is a rite of passage.

Arriving at a new posting with young children provides almost as many war stories. Expat women can and do sit around for hours, usually in an apartment compound or on a school playground, exchanging stories of hospitals, doctors, fathers who arrived at the last minute, and surreal deliveries the way other mothers exchange recipes. Living abroad with young children is a unique experience, and only other mothers in the same situation can relate.

Those overseas playground get-togethers are a lifeline of support. New mothers advise each other on breast-feeding, exchange the names of doctors, recommend great kids' clothing or toy stores, and can suggest where to find a nursing bra. They reassure each other that they are not alone in the experience of giving birth to and raising global nomads. Countless women have been through it and thrived. The babies, too. Since I was lucky enough to give birth to Lilly in Bangkok (nine months and two weeks after our arrival there), I have my own experiences to draw upon. While researching this chapter, I also communicated with an Australian spouse whom I knew had arrived at a recent posting in Southeast Asia in her first trimester of pregnancy with a toddler in tow. Listening to her stories and those of others made me realize that some things never change.

• *Making the decision to have a baby abroad*
The subject of expanding the family while living abroad (there are those unplanned pregnancies as well) merits a good deal of soul-searching and reflection. For instance, are you considering having a baby, or possibly a second child, primarily because there is available household help? Remember that, when you return to your home country, there probably won't be that kind of assistance at such a low price. The lovely Thai caregiver who helped me with Lilly teased me one day when I came home from the shops with another bucketload of bronze cutlery. "You won't have me around to polish that in Canada," she said. Her comment definitely sobered me up.

Deciding whether or not to have a baby is a serious matter wherever you happen to be living. When you are living abroad, nothing is normal. The family income may be higher, household help may be available, and any number of other factors will make your overseas life different from what you may be returning to in a few years.

• *Will yours be a potential high-risk pregnancy?*
As I was poring over the many excellent medical guides and websites aimed at travelers, one phrase kept showing up repeatedly: no pregnancy is normal until viewed after the fact. Nor should any woman overlook the statistics that up to 20 percent of pregnancies end in miscarriage within the first three months or the fact that between 15 and 20 percent of so-called low-risk pregnancies could require medical intervention of some type.

Is this your first pregnancy? Are you over the age of thirty-five? Do you have a previous history of obstetrical problems that may place this pregnancy at high risk? Do you have diabetes or hypertension? Is your pelvis small? Has an early ultrasound test revealed you are going to give birth to more than one baby? These are just a few questions to ask yourself when you become pregnant overseas.

In high-risk cases, doctors will usually point you in the direction of home. Your location itself may be considered "high risk" and unsuitable for deliveries. When we lived in Beijing, for instance, foreign women were discouraged from having their babies there due to the standard of the medical facilities. But life—and health care delivery abroad—have both improved considerably, allowing most women now to have their babies on posting.

• *Find a good place to live*
"The best thing we did when we arrived was to take our time finding the right place to live," my Australian friend wrote to me. "We chose extremely well as we live in a condo with 250 other families, of which 80 percent are expats and over half have children under the age of six...."

It gave me an instant network of support and resources from mothers who have all 'been there and done that' right here."

After the birth of her second child, this mother felt enormously guilty about the fact that her breast milk was drying up. She started chatting with another expat mom on the playground, who told my friend she had had the same problem because of the heat. "Instantly," my friend wrote, "I felt my guilt disappear. More to the point, I had the opportunity to have a conversation like that in the playground of my own condo building, which is something I really value and treasure. I have women supporting women right at my doorstep."

If you are renting a house, make sure it's a home that can be childproofed with gates. Have a look at the balcony if you are renting an apartment. And find something with enough room for a busy family. Overseas, your home often becomes an oasis from a foreign environment, so be sure to find somewhere you will want to spend time *en famille.*

- *Do you have medical insurance to cover hospital and other costs?*

If you haven't already explored the subject of medical insurance and benefits with your husband's employer, you had better begin. In some countries, having a baby can be a very expensive proposition. Find out what coverage you have for your doctors, medication, prenatal testing, hospitalization, and postpartum care. If the hospital standards are low where you are living, find out what the company will pay for outside of the country, including travel and accommodation before and after the arrival of the baby.

• *How to select an obstetrician and a hospital*

If you are considering pregnancy overseas, you will want to check out the local hospitals. Be sure to find out about C-sections, because sometimes these are unplanned. (I know that from personal experience.) What about blood supplies? Can the hospital handle a situation in which there is an Rh factor (that is, an incompatibility) involved? What is the pediatric staff like? Can the hospital accommodate premature babies? babies with heart defects? Is there a high-risk neonatal clinic? Go prepared with your list of questions. As for selecting an obstetrician, your best starting point is to talk to other expatriate women who have had babies where you are living. Simply ask them: who delivered?

When I was pregnant with Lilly in Bangkok, my Thai doctor had apparently delivered all the Canadian babies being born around that time. I actually arranged an appointment in his office *before* becoming pregnant to ask him all the questions I could think of, including: How often would I visit him? What would each visit involve? Where would I visit him? What tests would be required? Did he believe in using drugs during delivery?

All the while I was posing these questions, I was surreptitiously inspecting his diplomas. More than his paper qualifications, though, I was taking the measure of the doctor in whom I would place my trust for the next nine months and beyond. I was extremely fortunate; I knew almost immediately (from my own reaction and the testimonials of other expat women) that I was going to be in capable, reassuring hands. The doctor made me feel I had all the time in the world to discuss my future family. He did his best to answer my questions and to explain those areas with which I was unfamiliar. When we parted, he asked me to contact him if I had any problems with conception. Six weeks later, I faced him again—nauseous and embarrassed, yet extremely grateful—and he confirmed that I was pregnant.

• *How culture shock affects pregnancy*
Like everything associated with life overseas, the effects of pregnancy too can be amplified. I was barely used to my life as a *madame* in Bangkok when I became pregnant. Culture shock and pregnancy can produce a physical combination potent enough to depress and demoralize even the strongest of individuals, especially if prolonged morning sickness is part of it.

Getting used to being pregnant is not always easy. It's harder if the backdrop is unfamiliar and there is no mother or best friend around to talk to or hold your hand. You may sometimes feel you'll never have the nerve to walk out your door again. Getting around your new home base may be difficult, exacerbating feelings that you've lost your independence. Don't be alarmed. Usually, when the first trimester has passed and you can hold down a regular meal, it's amazing how much better you will feel about life in general and your pregnancy in particular.

• *Prenatal tests and training*
If you are thirty-five or over, amniocentesis is highly recommended to determine your baby's risk of genetic disorders. Depending on where you are living, this test may not be able to be done in-country. However, ultrasound equipment seems to be standard in most places. Typically,

your obstetrician will arrange for the regular blood and urine tests, and might recommend vitamin supplements. For readers going into remote areas, be prepared to travel for both consultations and tests.

The subject of prenatal tests raises the question of prenatal training. I'm talking here about those breathing lessons. Despite my own lessons, I failed miserably when the time came to use my skills. I even had a Thai midwife in a Bangkok hospital yell at me about my inability to breathe during contractions. I had enough air in me only to yell: "I believe in drugs!"

Obviously, your own doctor would be a good person to ask first about prenatal exercises. If there is a large modern hospital where you are living, the staff there may also be able to help you find a class. Encourage your husband to attend. These sessions are good not only for learning about the baby to come but for making new friends. This was the case for Rodney and me in Bangkok. From our prenatal group there also grew a large international mothers' support group that is still going strong.

• *Traveling while pregnant*
Decisions to travel during your pregnancy will depend on the stage you are at and the destination you have in mind. I made a very misguided decision to travel to Burma (Myanmar) in my seventh month of pregnancy. It was the most foolish thing I have ever done (and that's saying a lot), and I would recommend against any mother-to-be contemplating a similar foolhardy action. I was lucky nothing happened to either me or my baby. I'll use that embarrassing trip as an example of how *not* to travel during pregnancy, because it highlights the major issues

any pregnant woman should consider.

The first issue was that the Rangoon General Hospital would not have been my idea of a good place to give birth to my first child. Expat women living in Rangoon came to Bangkok at that time to have their babies, because of the lack of properly trained staff in Rangoon. The weather there was also overwhelmingly hot. In addition, the fresh water supply in our hotel was nonexistent, and the famous Shwe Dagon Pagoda (the tourist site not to be missed) has so many steps to be climbed that I realized halfway up them my complete miscalculation in being in Burma in the first place. Food was another story altogether. Let's just say that the dietary (and hygienic) requirements of a pregnant woman were not met.

A heartier traveler might have come through the same experience laughing (instead of crying and sweating, like I did), but my point is that common sense must prevail. I had clearly taken leave of mine because I was pregnant.

If you do fall into the "hearty" category and insist on traveling while pregnant, at least do it in the early stages, preferably during the second trimester when the more risky first three months are behind you. In the second trimester you can still see your toes, so you'll enjoy yourself more. Do go prepared with the names of doctors and hospitals should anything suspicious start happening to your body.

• *The delivery itself*

Long before the baby arrives, you and your obstetrician will have decided on the type of delivery that seems best.

You will have discussed the possibility of having drugs administered during labour, the idea of a spinal freeze (epidural), the use of a birthing room if one is available, precautions in the event of blood transfusions, and how long it might be necessary to stay in hospital.

I've listened to a lot of women talk about drug-free deliveries and all manner of what they consider the "natural" ways of producing a wished-for son or daughter. Having undergone an uncomfortable pregnancy and delivery by C-section under general anesthetic in Bangkok, I'd like to offer some advice: *do what is right for you.* Do not feel pressured by what other cultures or other women might be saying. A baby is a baby, and there are no judges standing around giving you marks for performance. My Australian friend concurs. "I was not interested in doing it the local way for the sake of assimilating, because I already felt under incredible pressure just from the relocation itself and coping with a new country, a husband who travels, and an eleven-month-old. I just wanted to reduce the stress in every possible way I could and, for me, that meant going Western. The stress of having a baby in another country is enough, in my opinion, without adding the pressure of feeling you have to re-invent the wheel."

Having a baby should at no time be a contest; nor should more expectations be heaped upon a pregnant woman than already exist by virtue of having a baby far from home. Choose the options that will work best for you.

SECURITY ISSUES

It is a fact of modern life that families living abroad who used to worry mainly about civil unrest in the host country now need to worry about random acts of terror. There is no way a parent can stop bad things from happening, but you can take control by having a family emergency plan in case something does happen and you need to round up everyone. Check with your children's school as well as with your company or sponsoring organization to find out what emergency contingency plans are already in place and fully acquaint yourself with those. Your family plan should include a location where you would all meet in the case of phone service being disrupted.

When Rodney and I were getting ready to move to Seoul in 1994, there was tension between the two Koreas, and newspaper editorials in the U.S. were scaring people, especially me. Rodney, as a political officer at our embassy, would be responsible for the evacuation of personnel and their families if things got really bad. This didn't reassure me in the least, for I reasoned we would be the last people out the door, turning out the lights as we went.

In the end, with all my attention focused on North Korea, I failed to consider that there could be infrastructure issues in the south, and that these would be a lot more dangerous than that standing army of one million just thirty-five kilometers away. During our first year in Seoul, a subway tunnel under construction exploded, a bridge fell down, a ferry burned, and a department store collapsed. In the event of an invasion from the north, we were all supposed to get ourselves to the U.S. army base.

Looking out onto the dead-end lane where we lived, where everybody not only double- but triple-parked, I had to laugh. There would be gridlock of the first order, and absolutely no one would be moving.

I guess the key lesson is try not to drive yourself and everyone around you crazy with worry. A sense of humour may be more helpful than a detailed evacuation plan, and keeping matters in perspective may be the greatest health tip of all.

Chapter 8

KEEPING YOUR FAMILY IN GOOD MENTAL HEALTH

Lois J. Bushong, MS, LMFT

THE WORLD HAS CHANGED since my missionary parents arrived on the coast of Central America in 1951 in a banana boat with three children under the age of four. Today, there are concerns for parents that were not a part of the landscape years ago. Expatriates of my parents' generation returned from distant countries with stories of diseases such as malaria, typhoid fever, and hepatitis. I never heard them discuss the emotional impact of an international assignment on their children, their marriage, or themselves.

The parents of today's global nomad are likely to be less apprehensive about disease than about keeping their children safe from kidnapping or armed robbery. They fear that their teenager will encounter problems with drugs, alcohol, sex, or peer pressure far from home. They worry that their child will someday walk out of a therapist's office convinced their life was ruined because their parents dragged them to the other side of the world.

As a child, I freely walked, roller-skated, and played on the sidewalk surrounding the presidential palace in Tegucigalpa, Honduras. When we lived outside the city, we spent hours riding horseback or hiking jungle trails looking for adventure. Today's parent would be strongly advised not to allow a daughter this freedom.

When I speak at transition workshops or to parents getting ready to launch their expatriate careers, I am often asked questions like the following: "What types of things should I be watching for in my child when we move overseas?" "Are there signs along the way that might indicate my son or daughter is not doing well with the move?" "What is normal behaviour?" Good questions. I'm glad parents are asking them rather than assuming all will be well.

As I was working on this chapter, I got a phone call from a friend in South America, telling me an armed man had just shot her teenage daughter in the leg before grabbing her cell phone and escaping in a waiting taxi. My friend was traumatized because she had been only a few feet away, helplessly witnessing the event. A scene like this can take place in any big city, but when it happens somewhere far from your support system, it will raise your anxiety level a few notches. My friend, besides wanting to reach out for the sound of my voice, wanted to know what she and her husband should be watching for in their daughter that would signal a need for counseling.

Because of groundwork done by past generations, there are many supports in place today for the global family, all aimed at making that international assignment a rich and enjoyable experience. Even with this support, you and your family will experience times that are very difficult as you make the transition to a new culture. That's normal. But how can you tell when you or someone in your family is experiencing problems that are deeper in nature? Here are some basic guidelines.

Whether it's counseling for your child, you and your

spouse, or yourself, don't wait until you are in crisis before you seek help. As with medical problems, it's better to check things out a bit too early rather than to procrastinate and then have to remedy a serious problem. At times, parents wait too long because they are embarrassed to seek assistance. But aren't your child, your marriage, and your life worth some possible embarrassment?

WHEN TO SEEK COUNSELING FOR YOUR CHILDREN

Expat parents frequently blame all of their children's negative behaviour on the family's mobility. But some of it may be attributable simply to growing up. Your children will move through the various developmental stages of challenging authority and wanting to be more independent whether you are living in the cornfields of Iowa or a remote village in Kenya. An international move can disrupt this normal process, and in the new context, the result might look almost delinquent. Keeping a sense of perspective about this may be enough.

Sometimes, however, your child might really be in trouble. Here are some signals I watch for when I work with children who live the nomadic life.

1. Excessive anger

If your child is throwing repeated temper tantrums, triggered by anyone and anything in their environment, it's time to pay attention. With small children, the anger may not be verbalized directly, but their disobedient behaviour will tell you they are angry. Some anger goes naturally with the developmental stage; "the terrible twos," for example, or teens at age fourteen. I'm talking here about an anger that just keeps on going, so that no one gets a break. You know your child. If his temperament changes dramatically, something has triggered this change, and you may need professional help to address it.

2. Academic problems

Some programs overseas have very high academic standards. If your child does not have a solid academic foundation, she is going to struggle in a new school of this kind. Instead of calling a therapist, you would be wiser to call on the services of a tutor. But if the new school's academic standards are similar to those of your child's previous school and your child's grades continue to drop, it's likely something major is distracting him or her. It's better to find out what is bothering your child early on than wait until the problem starts to affect them in other ways.

3. Other problems at school

It's a good idea to stay in contact with your child's main teacher. That person observes your child most of the day and can give you a heads-up if your child is being picked on by peers, isolating himself, being sent to the principal's office for disobedience, or spending a lot of time lost in a dream world. You do not want to stalk your child while they are at school, but neither do you want to ignore what is taking place there.

4. Depression

If you observe your child passing the weeks away sleeping, having no energy or interest in play, showing no appetite, crying a lot, or appearing withdrawn or just plain irritable, you probably have a child struggling with depression. If your child is a teenager, it's important to pay even closer attention, for teens tend to take matters into their own hands through using drugs, running away, and even fantasizing about suicide.

If you do seek therapy for your child's depression, be careful if the therapist suggests prescribing an antidepressant. In my practice, if I sense a child might need medication, I always send them to a psychiatrist who specializes in working with children. Medication of this kind can be dangerous for kids, and it should only be recommended by someone who really knows the field.

5. Refusal to communicate

Children and teens, just like adults, use various modes of escape from their problems. Some of the more common ones are spending too much time on the Internet, watching too much television, staying away from home for long periods, or locking themselves in their room whenever they are home. If this behaviour becomes excessive, and your child refuses to talk to you about what is going on, try to connect them with someone you trust and they feel comfortable with. I'd suggest you try another adult, maybe a teacher or family friend, before calling for an appointment with a counselor.

DRUGS, SEX, AND ALCOHOL

If you believe that an international assignment will protect your teen from having to deal with drugs, sex, and alcohol, you're in for a rude awakening. This is a problem right across cultures, and it can be heightened by the strict laws about drugs in some countries.

Barbara Berthiaume was an adolescent counseling consultant to international schools in Europe for twenty-four years. She informs me that many international schools have drug and alcohol awareness programs in which parents can learn about the rules of the country alongside their teens. Berthiaume notes also that in some countries parents could lose their work visa if a child becomes involved with drugs or other delinquent behaviour. Then there are countries like Holland, which take a very liberal view of marijuana use. Easy availability can cause problems, too.

"Parents need to keep the lines of communication open with their kids, be clear on their values, and set expectations for behaviour," Berthiaume says. "Even if there is not the availability of drugs in the host country, the teen will return home at some point and needs the information and social skills to deal with peer pressure."

WHEN TO SEEK MARRIAGE COUNSELING

Moving to a remote spot on the other side of the globe will naturally put stress on a marriage. As the family is throwing suitcases into the van on their way to the airport, it's normal to have a heated discussion about who packed the passports in which piece of carry-on baggage. And it must be decreed somewhere that it is a husband's duty to complain about the number of carry-on pieces as the family is checking through security. But if, after you've had months to settle into your new home, you overhear your children role-playing Mom and Dad fighting, it's time to sit down and have a serious discussion about what exactly is going on in your marriage.

Moving to another country can cause both partners in a couple to feel out of control, especially as they often have children for whom they feel a strong sense of responsibility. And if you have marital problems before you leave home, these are not going to lessen in a new country. If anything, they will escalate.

Some key signs that you need to consider marriage counseling include arguments that have become more frequent and more volatile; physical violence including shoving and slapping; an absence of physical intimacy; a working spouse finding all kinds of excuses not to be home; a spouse turning more frequently to an addiction like alcohol, golf, shopping, or the Internet; or a "cold war" in effect in the house in which the partners are not speaking to one another. The ideal is for the two of you to go together to counseling, but if your spouse refuses to go, start by going alone.

WHEN TO SEEK COUNSELING FOR YOURSELF

Mothers by their nature tend to spend much of their time looking out for and caring for the members of their family, sometimes neglecting their own mental health in the process. Here are some signs that you may need to seek personal counseling.

1. Depression

If you are experiencing feelings of hopelessness, cannot sleep, and have no motivation to get involved in activities that used to be of interest to you, you could be clinically depressed. Other symptoms of depression include ongoing sadness and/or tearfulness, withdrawal from society, and feelings of worthlessness. If these feelings have been going on for more then six months, they are not a phase of culture shock. If left untreated, depression can result in thoughts of hurting yourself or ending your life. Get help before you reach that stage.

2. Excessive anger

If you find that you are becoming more argumentative with your employer, your family, your spouse, your household help, or anyone within earshot, you should get some counseling. Some individuals get angry outwardly by ranting and raving, while others turn their anger inward, becoming depressed or developing ulcers or some other not-so-fun physical ailment.

When I ask expatriates how they made it through a particularly stressful adjustment to a new country, many begin by describing their strong support system. If you find yourself killing off your support system either with your anger or your silence, seek therapy so you can resolve what is going on beneath the surface. Otherwise, you risk finding yourself all alone many miles from home.

3. Heightened fear and anxiety

If, after the newness of the international move has worn off, you find yourself either with intense fear or no desire to venture outside the front door, you should consider getting some professional help.

I heard of one situation in which an expatriate family had been traumatized by an angry crowd while on an international assignment in Europe. After a short vacation that was supposed to calm the wife's nerves, the husband returned to his job, and all seemed to be functioning normally on the surface. But it turned out that the wife, who was home schooling their children, would not leave the safety of their house under any condition. Her husband covered for her while he went about his job, doing all the shopping and running of errands. They did not seek professional help, since they thought they could deal with the situation on their own. This couple is no longer living and working in Europe, and they are still working on repairing their marriage.

4. Behaviour that is getting you into trouble

I'm talking here about common addictions such as alcohol, drugs, sexual addiction, spending, food, and prescription pills. All of these are coping mechanisms to deal with pain you may be feeling beneath the surface. Get some help before your addictive behaviour destroys all that you have worked so hard to build.

5. Inability to function

Sometimes, an expatriate will find that he or she simply can't function anymore, either at work or on the home front. If you feel you have lost your focus, can't make decisions, are unable to do tasks you were able to do with ease in your home country, and are just existing from day to day, seek out some help.

6. Abnormal fatigue

The expatriate suffering from abnormal fatigue is not necessarily depressed, but spends more and more hours sleeping their life away or just staring at the four walls or mindlessly surfing the Internet. If this is you, and you come up with a clean bill of health after a comprehensive medical exam to check out your thyroid and any other possible medical issues, seek some counseling.

HOW DO YOU FIND A THERAPIST
ON THE OTHER SIDE OF THE WORLD?

This is a sensitive issue that needs to be handled in a confidential way, so here are some suggestions to help you.

1. Ask the local international community

Many expatriates are fearful of admitting they need help because of the possible negative impact on their career or their spouse's. If that's the case for you, be creative in how you obtain the information. There's always the old stand-by: "I have a friend in need of some counseling. Where should I recommend they get help?" Or try just listening to your friends: someone may mention a therapist they see. Word-of-mouth referrals are always best. When someone locates a good therapist, they often want to tell everyone about this wonderful person.

2. Ask your employer

Some international companies are very sensitive to the emotional needs of their employees and realize that people need some extra help from time to time. If your employer falls into that category, they may have the name of someone who helped their employees in the past.

QUESTIONS TO ASK PROSPECTIVE THERAPISTS

Here are some suggestions for questions to put to prospective therapists to find out if they will be a good match.

1. Have you ever lived in another country?

If so, ask how long and under what conditions? There is a big difference between being stationed in a country by the military, making a one-day layover on a cruise ship, volunteering with the Peace Corps, and living somewhere as a missionary. Someone once said that you do not totally understand what it is like to live overseas until you have no return ticket in your pocket and are hanging family pictures on the walls.

2. What is your background and training as a therapist?

I would recommend seeing a counselor with either a master's degree or a PhD. Does the therapist have a license in this new country or in your country of origin? Our field is sadly known for having a few counselors who do more damage than good, and licensure is one way to avoid this problem. You will want to look for a psychologist, a mental health counselor, or a marriage and family counselor. Some social workers are trained in counseling, too, but not all. Most psychiatrists are trained in dispensing medication but not in long-term counseling. Ask if you're unsure.

3. Do you have experience with or training in cross-cultural adjustment?

If the therapist you're interviewing does not have specialized training, is he or she interested in reading any resources on the topic? Are they willing to learn from you about the uniqueness of the global nomad? If they say the issue is not important, *run* elsewhere. Your life as an expatriate adds unique challenges to your psychological world, and these must be addressed.

Wherever we live in the world, there are adjustments to be made as a family moves through various developmental stages. The stress of living in another culture adds pressure to these normal transitions. The need to rebuild your support system and to adjust to new customs, cultures, ways of communicating, and foods, not to mention sleep cycles, can all affect individual psyches as well as family dynamics. What types of individual seem to thrive in an expatriate environment? Those who quickly bounce back after a crisis, are flexible, and do not carry a lot of emotional baggage. Families who possess an adventuresome spirit and have a good sense of humour do well with international assignments.

The life of the global citizen is fraught with danger and risks; it can be as frightening or as thrilling as riding a zip line through the rainforest in Latin America. For this global soul, my childhood years overseas were some of the happiest and hardest years of my life. I wish the same for your family.

Chapter 9

REPATRIATING GLOBAL NOMADS

WHENEVER I'M MAKING plans to speak about repatriation to parents at international schools, I know the topic will be a hard sell. Many expats are positively *repatriation-phobic;* they are not going to think about it *ever,* if they can avoid it. The feedback from organizers reflects another common attitude: if they are not repatriating in the next few months, many parents don't see the need to come and hear my talk. They couldn't be more wrong—a point they would learn if they came out to listen! Parents need to be aware of the repatriation challenges that lie ahead for their global nomads *throughout* the overseas experience.

Preparations for the day your children will return "home" should not be left to the last minute. Life skills acquired along the way can ease a child's transition not only to the culture stamped on his passport but also to a future life as a productive and happy adult, ready to assume his place in the world. What's more, *everyone* in your expat community is affected by repatriation, even if yours doesn't happen to be the family moving. Why? Because you can be sure that one of your children's best friends or favourite teachers is moving. That's the reality of expatriate life. Someone is always moving on.

As moving season creeps up each year, you will look around your dinner table to see children of all ages wearing long faces. If your kids are the ones about to move, they may be wondering why their friends suddenly seem to be withdrawing from them. A period of disengagement is common as children protect themselves by stepping back from someone close to them who is leaving. Teenagers have been known to break off their relationships months before the school year ends if one or the other in the couple learns they will be leaving. Young girls start weeping in advance over a cherished friend who is moving, worrying they will never see each other again. There's always one youngster (usually a boy) who figures going home will be a breeze, because naturally he'll play football or basketball on the senior school team. This guy's living in denial, a place we've visited often throughout these pages. He's blissfully unaware his new classmates may have spent years working toward the goal of making a varsity team.

Most expatriate adults have learned to accept the springtime moving period as a natural part of the expatriate life cycle, much like a change of season. It simply marks the inevitable passage of time. In the transient expatriate world, though, time easily slips into hyper drive. During a two-year time period, a family can arrive in a place unknown, quickly make friends, make better friends with people who become close friends, then see those close friends become friends living somewhere else in the world—all in the blink of an eye.

Transition is not a notion easily grasped by children, who live in the here and now. Kids don't understand life cycles. After all, they have had so few. In the time before their own move or that of their best friends, they may be sad, angry, depressed, relieved (if they have hated where you live), or excited. Sometimes, they'll experience all of these emotions at once.

Nor do children understand that things usually work out in the long term. Patience is not a virtue common to them. So this is where you, the parent, come in. You must help your children manage the expectations and fears that are part of the transition to their "passport" culture. As Dave Pollock and Ruth Van Reken point out in *Third Culture Kids*, for a great number of TCKs the re-entry process more closely resembles an *entry* (my italics). That means a brand-new job is just beginning for you, the parent. At the same time, you are managing your own feelings about moving home.

WHY IS YOUR FAMILY REPATRIATING?

The decision to move a family home is usually made by others. One possible cause is that the company or organization that has offered the overseas assignment is ending the job or sending the employee back into the system at headquarters. This kind of repatriation, while challenging, is nevertheless straightforward. Many families, though, are told they will be going home without an actual departure date attached. This uncertainty can become the source of much tension as the mother tries to plan the move and get her children signed up for schools in the next location.

Other common reasons for going home include retirement (in which case, children are probably grown up and no longer an issue), a change of career, or the ill health of a family member. As I've said earlier, divorce and separation happen often in the expat world, too, and a mother may set off for home with the children, leaving the father behind. In these unfortunate circumstances, counseling will be useful for everyone. It is hard enough for children to reintegrate into the home culture without the family configuration changing, too. Equally emotionally exhausting for the family can be decisions based on the needs of the children. In our own case, for example, we decided we wanted Lilly to begin high school in Canada. A child may also have special education needs that are not being met in the international school system. Finally, it may be as simple as this: a family is not happy living overseas.

Regardless of why the decision is taken to go home, the way you as parents handle the move will be critical for your children. Let's examine some of the challenges and discuss ways you can help your children move through the transition.

EVERYONE IS CHANGED BY AN OVERSEAS EXPERIENCE

When I was still a meticulous picture taker and home-movie auteur, I was able to handily pull out evidence that the children who'd arrived at post were definitely not the same ones leaving. Physical growth spurts were only the outward manifestation of just how much the kids had changed while we were living in Taipei or Seoul. The story on the inside—their experiences learning alongside classmates from all over the globe; traveling to nearby countries and engaging in local festivals and holidays; coming to know the sound of other languages and the taste of exotic fruit—was the one I would try to articulate for my children. It was important that they understood they had changed as human beings. It wasn't just a matter of growing up. Their outlook on the world had grown wider.

I felt this was a necessary discussion before my family went home, and I believe other parents getting their children ready for repatriation would be well advised to engage in some of these conversations. The more children *know* themselves, the more confident they will feel. They may not show or express it in words, or even understand it on a conscious level, but this self-knowledge will help carry them through some insecure days settling into a new place.

It's also very important to remind your children that the world hasn't stopped while they have been away. Adults, too, often make the mistake of returning home with the attitude that *they* are the only ones who have changed or, indeed, had life-altering experiences. As I have explained to audiences when I speak about repatriation, conversation should always be a two-way proposition. *Everyone* has changed in some way, and each person should get a chance to speak.

Expat parents and children can also feel upon re-entry that people are pushing them aside and ignoring them, shutting out their traveler's tales. Based on my own experience, I think expats arrive home on the margins and need to proactively work their way back into the mainstream. Children will do this in very different ways from their parents, since global nomads feel like different people when they return. They look the same as everyone else, though (which is why they have been described as "hidden immigrants"), and they don't want to be seen as different. For that reason, they are often the last ones to spill the beans about having lived abroad. They certainly don't want to be *seen* as showing off by talking about this or that foreign country or exotic holiday the family had at Christmas.

I used to arrange a meeting with my children's new teachers before they returned to Canadian schools to specifically ask that the children *not* be singled out in a way that would upset them. It was all right to say they had just joined the class, but tacking on "Jay just moved here from Korea. Jay, speak to us in Korean" would have killed my son with embarrassment. Kids just want to fit in, even if it means hiding a huge chunk of their lives.

YOUR FEELINGS ABOUT THE RE-ENTRY AFFECT YOUR CHILDREN

If moving home is not making you happy, and the reason for the repatriation happens to be your children's needs (or your perception of those needs), stop and consider how letting your kids know this will affect them. Of course they will see themselves as the source of your unhappiness. Likewise, if divorce is the reason you're moving home, and your children had been happy where they were living, there could be double-barreled anger directed at you as parents, both for splitting up and for messing up your kids' lives abroad. Divorce is never easy, but in expatriate circumstances a family breakup can be even more intense for children.

As in my own case, mothers who are thrilled about repatriating (and are working with some false expectations) may be waxing poetic about "home" when that place is somewhere the children have never lived. When we moved from Seoul to Vancouver, Vancouver certainly wasn't home in the true sense of the word. We knew the airport well from years of transfers through there, but the city itself was just somewhere beautiful with mountains that we knew from postcards. There was a heap of denial going on in my head about what life on the west coast of Canada would be like, far from my comfort zone of friends and family in central Canada. When reality caught up with me—and I write about the fatigue and depression I experienced in my book *Homeward Bound*—I passed a lot of my distress and unhappiness along to my kids. I wish I could take back so many of my "bad hair" days now.

Repatriation also means a major change in your living circumstances. Life may become a lot more modest at home (no cars with drivers or exotic getaways at holidays). Much of your shock as a parent may come with the realization that you have to let your children enjoy some new freedom after coming from the essentially gated expat communities. In the real world of "home," adult supervision at other children's houses, for example, may suddenly seem to have vanished, because single-parent families (with the single parent out working a lot of the time) are more commonplace. If they are teenagers, your children may quickly become outraged at the idea of a parent even being at home when they plan to throw a party. When we first moved to Vancouver, Lilly couldn't get enough of the public transit system. She pored over bus schedules in her free time. It didn't matter if she actually needed to go anywhere; to her, the ability to take a bus meant a level of independence she had never enjoyed before. Naturally, I fretted over the idea of her alone on a bus, but I finally recognized that since she was thirteen, I couldn't reasonably hold her back.

Your children need the opportunity to build new relationships and friendships as well as to establish new interests. It means cutting them some slack emotionally, too. Some days will definitely be better than others. One day you will say good morning to a child and receive a loving smile back; the next day, the smile is replaced with "What's good about it?" These mood shifts are easier to take if you're prepared for them.

RE-ENTRY SHOCK

Everyone living abroad has some idealized version of "home," which is often rooted in the past. As you contemplate your move from a tropical country back to one with snow, you may conveniently forget that the snow lasts six months, not six hours. Relationships with siblings, parents, and friends that were so easy over e-mail may be more difficult in person. Your country, as well as your friends and family, may have changed. As your vision of home collides with the reality, you will encounter re-entry shock.

Re-entry shock is simply the reverse culture shock you experience in your own country when you visit places that should be familiar to you, but aren't; try to interact with people you should feel comfortable with, but don't, or face situations you should be able to handle, but can't. As I wrote in *Homeward Bound*, "Re-entry shock is when you feel like you are wearing contact lenses in the wrong eyes. Everything looks almost right."

HOW DOES A CHILD EXPERIENCE RE-ENTRY SHOCK?

A child's re-entry shock will follow a similar pattern to an adult's, although it probably won't last as long; a parent's re-entry shock can be eighteen months to two years in duration. The stages of re-entry shock are similar to those of culture shock itself: a honeymoon period, crisis, flight, and readjustment. Both children and adults may experience symptoms such as anxiety, alienation, insomnia, and depression. Mood swings for both child and parent are inevitable. The best you can hope for is that your family rides the same mood cycle, though it's not likely that will always be the case.

Anger is very common among children during re-entry shock, and, interestingly, that anger can be directed not only at family but also at new peers. "At times it seems TCKs can be culturally tolerant anywhere but in their own culture," write Pollock and Van Reken in *Third Culture Kids*. "When people move to a new host culture, they usually keep quiet if they have strongly negative opinions about that culture. At most, they only express them to fellow expatriates. The rules seem to change, however, on re-entry. Some TCKs appear to feel quite free to express every negative opinion they can possibly think of about their home culture, no matter who is around."

Therapist Lois Bushong makes an important point about re-entry. "Parents should remember that 'home' is a new country to their children. So it helps when parents try to recall their feelings as they initially adjusted overseas to a country they didn't know. They will better empathize with what their children are feeling."

WHY CAN RE-ENTRY BE MORE CHALLENGING FOR CHILDREN?

My son, Jay, put it best after his first day at a new elementary school when we repatriated to Vancouver. When I asked him if most of the kids knew each other from kindergarten, he said, "Mom, these kids have been playing together since they were in diapers!" He wasn't kidding.

We had moved into a neighbourhood where new kids on the block were rare. That made it tough for our young son, who didn't socialize as easily as his older sister. It's something to keep in mind when you choose where you'll live upon repatriation. Will it be back in a neighbourhood where you are known and your children may still have a few friends? Or will you be trying a new city?

As I outlined in chapter 3, the hidden losses of global nomads can result in unresolved grief. The losses they experience on repatriation include the loss of their former status and way of living, the loss of travel opportunities, and the loss of friends and other important relationships. Compounding this sense of loss is the fact that returning global nomads are often not allowed to grieve, or even to talk about their feelings. "Successful adjustment to a new location depends upon bringing appropriate closure to the old," says transition expert Barbara Schaetti. "Some families may feel uncomfortable saying good-bye and attending to other such closure activities. It's too 'touchy feely'; they don't know what to do with the emotion that inevitably gets stimulated; they're too busy and can't afford the time it takes. In reality, families can't afford not to take the time."

Your role as a repatriating parent may mean helping your children (young and old) to say good-bye to their friends as well as to the places they have frequented. You may also need to intervene in helping them to bring outstanding disputes to some resolution before you move. If a child learns that he can walk away from a dispute (whether it's with a friend or a teacher), then a pattern—and not a healthy one—may become well established before adulthood.

"Some global nomads do not grieve the transition back to their passport [home] culture until later in their lives, when another life event can trigger all of those pent-up emotions," notes therapist Bushong. "The delayed response is due either to denial at the time or because they needed every ounce of emotional energy to adjust to college life in the 'new' country. Those feelings may also have been too hot to touch at that moment. So the emotions hit later. The age of twenty-eight or later, or when life has settled down, seems to be a time when an adult global nomad may suddenly get angry or experience grief from all the losses they hid or denied."

REPATRIATING TEENAGERS WHO ARE OFF TO COLLEGE

Going "home" is trying at the best of times, but for an expatriate teenager bound for college whose home has technically been wherever his nomadic parents happened to be living at the moment, it can be even more challenging. That's one of the reasons I'm especially pleased to be invited to speak to repatriating seniors at international schools, although often, like their parents, the soon-to-be-graduates don't see any need to talk about it.

I almost gave up speaking to teenagers altogether after I was invited to do a two-hour workshop with a senior class living in an Asian capital. To me, this particular group of young adults exemplified the dark side of kids who grow up with an inflated sense of entitlement and heightened self-esteem. Their arrogance and rudeness were so off-putting I could barely contain myself. I confess, I did lose my cool entirely when one young girl stood up and announced point-blank: "I don't need to be here!"

"Oh, I guess I'm mistaken," I said. "You've already

been to university. You have already felt re-entry shock and the isolation of being over there while your parents are over here. And of course you know how to find your way around a large campus where you have simply become a number."

"Well, no, I haven't been to university yet," she said, backing down a bit. "And no, I don't believe I've ever experienced re-entry shock." She started to take her seat, but not before I barked out: "Then sit down and listen. Sometimes the adults know a thing or two."

I never perform well when I'm outraged, and this particular group's behaviour had pushed me to the limits. My antipathy had actually started on the airplane (I flew with the group on one of their study holidays in order to squeeze in my lecture) when not one but two different teenagers insisted they wanted my seat on the airplane to be near a friend. I was dizzy from playing musical chairs before the plane even left the gate.

When the workshop had mercifully ended—and unsatisfactorily, in my view—I was convinced I had overstepped my boundaries. That is, until the teenagers' teachers surrounded me and led me straight to the bar in the hotel where we were staying. They insisted on buying me several rounds, saying I deserved it. Indeed, they thanked me for telling off the kids, because apparently their parents rarely did. Despite that irritating group—which thankfully has been counterbalanced by several more thoughtful and respectful groups—I believe the need to educate teenagers about re-entry remains critical. Note to guidance counselors: For a talk I gave in the U.K. once, a marvelous high school counselor got on the school loudspeaker and told all seniors to report to the auditorium, without telling them why. Everyone showed up, and one of the seniors came up to me afterwards and said, "That really resonated with me."

Paul Maxfield, a co-founder of Families in International Transition (FIT), an organization that helps parents on the move, believes that global nomads heading off to college need coaching on some practical life skills. "Lifestyle, domestic help, lack of work opportunities, and cultural practices all contribute to a lack of life skills and experience that teenagers will feel when they are living on their own," says Maxfield. "Graduating teenagers should be given a self-assessment (and preferably before their senior year) that covers general skills that will be needed."

Managing money probably ranks highest on the list of much-needed skills for independent living. Young adults need to learn what things cost, how to save money, and how to budget. Otherwise, they will get to college and run through enormous sums of money in the blink of an eye. As I noted in chapter 4, parents don't need to wait until children are ready to leave home to teach them about money.

Another big challenge for returning teenagers, according to FIT's Maxfield, can be assuming responsibility for their behaviour and actions. Growing up, the role models for global nomads may have been parents and other adults who were always around to do things for them or to intervene on their behalf. Do you want your child to grow up always blaming someone else for his mistakes or having you, the parent, intervene? Or, worse, blaming you for everything that has gone wrong in their lives? If you never allow your children to clean up mistakes for themselves, their strength of character will never develop.

When one of Jay's high school friends got a second-hand car with a stick shift for graduation, all his friends were pleased for him. They also loved to sit back and watch as this guy constantly stalled his car. One summer evening, Jay came running in the door with the bad news that, while fooling around in his friend's car, he had taken off the emergency brake without allowing enough time for his friend to get the car started. You can guess what happened. The car rolled down the street—hitting his friend's parents' car! Although his friend might have taken some responsibility (it was his car, after all), Jay insisted that he had not given his pal enough time to recover from the stall. ("Even ten more seconds would have helped, Mom," he explained sadly to me.) So he marched back over to his friend's house, told his friend's parents that it was *his* fault, and pledged to pay the significant amount of money for the repairs. "Easy come, easy go" was the phrase we heard from our son's mouth soon afterwards; he had just resold a video camera he had saved money to buy for the exact sum he needed to pay for his moment of madness. We've never been prouder of him.

Repatriation is a challenge for everyone in the family, and it's wise to do some research on this important part of the expatriate life cycle long before you and your children find yourselves in the throes of it. My book *Homeward Bound* is full of advice on making your family's repatriation successful.

Chapter 10

TRANSFORMING GLOBAL NOMADS INTO GLOBAL CITIZENS

I BEGAN WRITING this book in earnest in the middle of a record-breaking rainy January in Vancouver. Every morning, I headed off to a quiet room at the local library, my salvation from the distractions in my home office: the telephone, the Internet, the laundry, a crazy barking dog, and the mood swings of a recently returned college-grad daughter trying to figure out her next move.

One morning during that dark month, Lilly needed to be dropped at the airport to catch a flight to central Canada. After finishing her degree and living at home for five months, she had scored an internship with an environmental nongovernmental organization in Ottawa. She was officially happy once more. Not surprisingly, she was also on the move again.

Her five-month transition period had held way too many ups and downs for me. I wasn't used to having my daughter around full time anymore. The space I had cleared in my head for other matters when she went off to college suddenly was filled again with details of her life. There were a thousand minimum-paying jobs to discuss, cover letters to check for her as she responded to ads in the paper and on the Internet, and too many conversations about relationships.

For the first time in Lilly's life, all was not obvious and clear-cut. I think that was the biggest shock to her system—and to her parents, too. Despite my own best efforts to convince her that sometimes *not* knowing the future is a good thing, she had still required high-maintenance emotional support during many teary days. I wasn't worried about her in the long term, since her environmental passion, her commitment to helping others, and her focus and propensity for hard work will all serve her well. Lilly also knows who she is and what she wants to achieve in her life: she just needed to be a bit more patient. So did her mother.

Nonetheless, I was really going to miss her, and I braced myself for our farewell scene at the airport. Memories of the first time I had left her, outside a college dorm in Halifax, ran through my mind. I had been choked up then, too. Fortunately, Lilly brought a little levity to the occasion.

"Don't take this the wrong way, Mom," she said, giving me a big hug as we unloaded the trunk of the car. "But I hope I don't come home again, except for the holidays."

"That's all right, sweetie," I said. "Don't *you* take this the wrong way, but I also hope you don't move home again." She scooped up the few bags she was taking and vanished into the unknown, which that morning was suitably represented by a busy airport terminal. Driving away, I burst into tears. My global nomad daughter—determined to save the planet—was well on her way to becoming a global citizen.

WHAT IS GLOBAL CITIZENSHIP?

"Global citizenship is a way of thinking and behaving," according to Oxfam, which provides a wonderful website full of resources to help teachers introduce the idea into the classroom. "It is an outlook on life, a belief that we can make a difference." Well, no arguments from me that my daughter, her friends locally and around the world, and so many of the children I meet in my travels definitely fit that description.

According to Oxfam's profile, a global citizen holds to the ideals every expat parent wishes for their global nomad. Global citizens and global nomads share many traits.

- They are aware of the wider world and have a sense of their role as world citizens.
- They respect and value diversity.
- They have an understanding of how the world works economically, socially, politically, culturally, technologically, and environmentally.
- They are outraged by social injustice.
- They participate in and contribute to the community at a range of levels, from local to global.
- They take responsibility for their actions.

A good friend of mine, an American living in London, wrote to me about this issue. "As the world grows ever smaller, and technology paves the way for faster and more easily accessible connections and networks, astute parents of global nomads can no longer be satisfied with raising children to think of themselves simply as nomads, content only to observe and imbibe the cultures and countries in which they live." The mother of two global nomads, she has been a tireless volunteer in every international school

197

her children attended. Like I do, she feels that volunteerism and citizenship are at long last blending together:

"I believe that, as parents, we have the opportunity and the responsibility to raise our global nomads to become active global citizens," my friend continued. "Having lived in more than one community or country, these children understand that the *world* is their home and that good citizenship extends beyond borders. For the global nomad, good global citizenship translates into feeling connected and at home in the world."

Global nomads need to emerge from their childhoods happy and healthy, though, in order to put the benefits of a childhood abroad to use for the advantage of everyone. A sense of global citizenship won't happen automatically. In other words, like everything else I've written about, it will require a considerable investment of parents' time and energy.

GLOBAL NOMADS IN THE WORKING WORLD

As the world of commerce becomes integrated internationally, who better to provide business with global sensitivity than employees who have spent their childhoods in an overseas milieu? "The global nomad life does provide the opportunity for children and adolescents to cultivate certain perspectives and skills without conscious volition," says Barbara Schaetti. "It's those perspectives and skills, as a total package, which global nomads are likely to offer their employers."

According to Schaetti's research, global nomads bring valued traits such as the following: multifaceted backgrounds, which enable a match between global nomad employees and individual client personalities, an important element in client relationships; a broad world-view and the skills to deal with cross-cultural experiences on many different levels; the empathic abilities and experience in bridging differences that make them good mediators and cultural brokers; language skills, and experience with change, a critical skill in today's business environment.

"There are lots of people today who see the world with a broadened perspective and demonstrate flexibility," Schaetti believes. "But those who have grown up across cultures while moving internationally will also demonstrate a confidence and a comfort in the face of ambiguity. They bring to business the ability to look for deeper levels of meaning and to question assumptions."

One adult TCK, who grew up as a diplomat's daughter, puts it this way: "I can walk into a new situation or a new country and know how to stand back and listen so that I can find out how people operate. I can suspend judgment when a situation or behaviour seems strange, and wait for an explanation to suggest itself rather than judge immediately. I have the ability to live with questions and with 'not knowing.' "

However, before children can launch into the working world and maximize the opportunities created by their upbringing, they must be ready to leave home. And it's parents who are responsible for preparing them properly.

DELAYED ADOLESCENCE

Parents with youngsters under thirteen are probably too distracted by diapers or soccer practice to think as far ahead as launching *anyone.* If your children are adolescents, though, read on. A critical barrier to that successful launch could be the delayed adolescence I first raised in chapter 1 and, with that, rebellion that has been postponed.

"A delayed adolescence is painful enough for the TCK who keeps wondering why he or she can't be like others, but even more painful—not only for TCKs but for their families as well—is a delayed adolescent rebellion, a time when the normal testing of rules either starts unexpectedly late or becomes exaggerated in an all-out, open defiance of nearly every possible convention the family and/or community holds dear and extends far beyond the adolescent years," write Dave Pollock and Ruth Van Reken in *Third Culture Kids.*

Loneliness certainly plays a part in this: teenage rebellion has been known through the ages as a plea for attention or help. The problem when a TCK acts up is that the behaviour may occur long after the teen years have ended and carry more serious consequences, like walking away from a marriage and children. A rebelling adult global nomad may say: "I've spent my life making everyone else happy. Now it's my turn."

Pent-up anger is the major culprit in this situation, and it is usually aimed at parents. According to Pollock and Van Reken, once young adults no longer need to comply, they may want to do everything they couldn't do while under the restraints that went with their role in an expat community. The anger at parents can easily mutate into blame if the struggle to regain their equilibrium lingers on. Naturally, these young adults believe they wouldn't be struggling to find their way if only they had led a normal life—without moves. And we all know who was responsible for the relocations. Children who feel this way will want to hurt their parents.

To avoid rebellion that results from children feeling everything was predetermined for them, parents would do well to create opportunities early on for their children to make real choices in certain matters—and for them to experience the real consequences that result from those choices. This exercise definitely does not need to wait until repatriation.

Muddying the waters of delayed rebellion is the twenty-first-century adolescent ethos. At its core, it places a huge value on celebrity (making fame the holy grail) and has a mantra that cries "30 is the new 21." This philosophy can make it difficult to see clearly if your young adult is part of this group who never intends to grow up or is just experiencing the residue of the global childhood.

Every parent wants their child to have a healthy sense of self-esteem. But don't go overboard in encouraging it to compensate for the unique circumstances of living and moving abroad. That could make happiness as an adult elusive for your child.

HELP YOUR CHILDREN KNOW THEMSELVES

There's a saying that we spend our adulthoods getting over our childhoods. Nowhere does this cliché apply more than to the global nomad whose parents have not prepared him well enough for adulthood or taught her how to take responsibility for her own actions.

Mel Levine, in his book *Ready or Not, Here Life Comes*, writes that work-life unreadiness is rampant in today's society. Dr. Levine, as I noted earlier, does not write with an expatriate audience in mind, but many of his sage words of advice and the tips he offers may be helpful to expat parents preparing their young adults for a successful launch into the real world.

"Knowledge of one's background, personal strengths, weaknesses, tastes, and disinclinations helps immeasurably in charting a course for the startup years," he writes. "Knowing who you are makes knowing what to do a whole lot easier and more satisfying.... Parents and teachers have to encourage this line of thinking and talking, since so many kids never experience it."

Dr. Levine does not address the specific questions of identity that plague the global nomad, including the dreaded "Who am I?" and "Where am I from?" But anything related to issues of identity and self-knowledge is potentially dangerous territory for a young person. As parents of global nomads, you will have to play a greater role in helping your children understand themselves, whether it's giving them talking points when they are younger or providing more mature coping mechanisms for the complexities resulting from their peripatetic childhoods.

Ruth Van Reken, in her recent research on cross-cultural kids, advises parents to remind expat children that they are persons, like everyone else, before they are TCKs; to look for ways (counseling, testing, conversations) to help children identify their particular gifts, personality, and skills; to develop a strong sense of family identity and belonging, and, finally, to remind children that they don't have to reject either the past or the present to preserve the other—they can be both/and. It's essential they take ownership of their experience. Barbara Schaetti's commentary on global nomad identity development expands on this.

Self-assessments and skills inventories should be

done in a context of optimism. It can be as simple as me reminding my son, as he prepared to go to high school, that he had a track record of success. Dr. Mel Levine suggests that parents take every opportunity to reinforce this idea by sharing stories from their own childhood of times when keeping a positive attitude paid off.

Of course, too much optimism can also be an issue, which is why reality checks are equally important. The risky flip side of fueling our children with too much self-confidence, a point parenting experts have been making during the past decade, has been that some children truly do feel they can do, and are entitled to do, anything—regardless of whether they have the aptitude or proper skills.

WHEN CHILDREN LEAVE THE HOME

The empty-nest syndrome has been well documented. The term describes a time when parents—mothers in particular—feel bereft at the loss of a child who is in transition to adulthood and independence. For expatriate parents and families, the emotional leave-taking can be particularly challenging.

"Expat families often say that moving around has made them closer, and they rely more on each other and on the family unit for support," says Phyllis Adler, an American counselor and coach who works with expatriates in London. "When one person leaves, that dynamic is changed. A parent's relationship with their child is now compounded by the great distance thrown up between them, and the inability to be near when needed. The expat life exacerbates the situation, as it seems to do with most stress."

Expat mothers in the middle of a move themselves may find empty-nest syndrome even more difficult to cope with. They may be increasingly lonely abroad without their children around. But Adler reminds women to "never forget that you are still needed. The bond has not been broken, simply matured." She offers more good advice to expat women who have given up an established work identity and structured their lives around their families: find an activity or outlet to replace the pieces of identity that are lost when your child moves; use this stage of life in a positive manner to reinforce your marriage, by finding time to have more fun together, perhaps by traveling; give yourself positive reasons for your day, every day. Most women dream of an entire day to themselves to read a book, paint, walk, or work. Now you can make that happen.

Finally, says Adler: "Remember that the best gifts you can give your child may be the gifts of a positive attitude, courage, and trust in them to find their life now."

Travel writer, essayist, and global soul Pico Iyer has written that "global citizenship does not mean giving up a sense of roots so much as extending our sense of what roots involve." It is my belief that parents ground their children with roots made of love and respect. The family's values, beliefs, and traditions are like the branches of a tree; the enriched childhood produces colourful foliage. Some leaves may appear later than others, but that's fine, too. It takes a lot of trees to create a forest, just as so many unique cultures make up our world.

Nurturing young people is never more critical than when you are living abroad. Help your children to become sturdy, to take sustenance in the roots of your family and the experiences you share. Assist them as they negotiate the inevitable obstacles that block their paths, but make them do the heavy lifting. Then you can stand back and watch your children thrive, secure in the knowledge that you have done your very best in raising your global nomad.

A MOST EXCELLENT JOURNEY

Barbara F. Schaetti, PhD

THE TYPICAL GLOBAL NOMAD travels extensively. Passports fill with stamps, photo albums fill with images of exciting adventures, and lifelong personal and family memories are made. For many global nomads, as it was for me as the daughter of an oil executive, jumping on an airplane headed to some far-flung destination is as normal as getting in a car to drive across town.

There is one journey, however, that is unlike any other a global nomad will make. More than that, it is a journey that all global nomads must undertake. What I'm talking about here is the journey of identity development. Although it's a passage your global nomad children have to negotiate on their own, it's one that you as the parent can significantly influence and support.

DEFINING "IDENTITY" AND "IDENTITY DEVELOPMENT"

For our purposes here, "identity" is simply the sense of who each of us is—as a person, as a part of a family and a community, and as a contributing member of society. Identity is largely unconscious, but determines how we draw our boundaries, how we decide who is "me, not you," "we, not them." Identity is about inclusion and exclusion.

"Identity development" is the search for congruence in our sense of who we are. We need to resolve any differences between who we think we are now, who we once thought ourselves to be, who others perceive us to be, and who we want to become. In order to do this, we consciously explore our boundaries. Is this about me, or is this about you? Who is included in my group, who is not, and how has that changed?

In the early days of identity research, identity was understood to be based on groupings like family and kinship systems, nationality, ethnicity, race, and language. More recently, it has also been recognized as relating to gender, age, sexual orientation, immigration or refugee status, socioeconomic status, religious or spiritual orientation, political orientation, physical ability, and more.

Identity development usually begins by mid to late adolescence, around one or another of these identity groupings. Before that we may be female but not have thought about gender, Muslim but not have thought about religion, light-skinned but not have thought about race. At some point, something happens that brings a particular group and our place within it to our conscious awareness. And so for months, sometimes even for years, we deliberately explore our relationship to that grouping.

THE IDENTITY WEB

As we progress through adulthood, we typically have experiences that cause us to consider our relationship to a lot of different groups. Our mature identity is rooted in a uniquely woven web of groupings that give meaning to whom we know ourselves to be.

Some people have more choice than others about which groupings they explore. The more distinct you are from the mainstream, through appearance or experience, the more groupings you will likely weave into your identity web. If you have grown up racially different from the majority, for example in terms of either numbers or of power/privilege, you'll no doubt find yourself confronting issues of race.

You can see that this gives a kind of "identity privilege" to people who are part of the majority in any grouping. If you're white growing up in a white-majority country, you have the privilege of not having to think about race. If English is your mother tongue and you live in an English-speaking environment, you have the privilege of not having to learn another language.

However, being in the majority is also a real disadvantage. Allowed the luxury of ignorance, we all too often stay ignorant. Identity development has the potential to teach us self-reflection and to strengthen our capacity to creatively engage with complexity. It expands our capacity to be successful in a multifaceted and constantly changing world.

IDENTITY DEVELOPMENT FOR GLOBAL NOMADS

The identity webs of global nomads are deeply influenced by their internationally mobile childhoods. Once they leave the expatriate environment, they no longer have the "luxury of ignorance." Instead, to one extent or another, they start to consider the consequences—to their values, beliefs, ways of being, and ways of doing—of their global childhood experiences.

Most of the early research on global nomads focused

on identity *outcomes,* describing the typical cultural characteristics of global nomads once they had reached adolescence and/or adulthood. In general, these outcomes are strongly positive—at least, most global nomads, by the time they reach adulthood, are able to work through the negative dimensions of the global nomad experience and maximize the positive ones. As Robin declares early in this book, "Most children turn out great!"

Well, yes and no. Most global nomads do successfully integrate their mobile childhoods into their adult identities and become happy and contributing members of society. Some, however, get stuck in years of unnecessary pain and anguish. Focusing on global nomad identity in terms of identity *development* can help to explain the difference. It can also reveal some points of attention for proactive parenting.

THE STAGES OF IDENTITY DEVELOPMENT

Global nomads of my generation (mid-forties or older) came to know ourselves more by instinct than by conscious intention. No one told us that we were on a journey called "global nomad identity development." No one knew. We were pretty much on our own, left to sink or swim. Now, that has changed. So here's the first key strategy for parents: know that there is a road map, be sure you understand the general gist of it yourself, and give your children information about it as and when they're ready.

Global nomads go through five stages of identity development in their search for congruence. These are (1) pre-encounter, (2) encounter, (3) exploration, (4) integration, and (5) recycling. Let's take a closer look at each of these. A note before we start: Although identity explorations in one grouping influence whether, when, and how we search for identity congruence in others, in this commentary I'm going to separate global nomad identity from the rest.

1. Pre-encounter

Pre-encounter is the period before identity exploration begins. Global nomads are just living their internationally mobile lives, not thinking about how those lives are shaping who they are. Yet it's their experiences during this time that ultimately fuel their search for identity congruence. Historically—and by that I mean for the global nomads of my generation—the pre-encounter period ran into adolescence, sometimes even into young adulthood.

2. Encounter

One day, the global nomad will have an experience that wakes her up to the fact that she is different from others specifically because of growing up globally. If your children, like me, were born overseas or moved overseas at a young age, they won't remember a time when they weren't different. Being different is for them a normal part of everyday life. At some point, however, something will cause them to recognize that difference in a new, more conscious way. This kind of "encounter" forces us into self-reflection: we become curious about who we are and about how and why we move through the world in the way we do.

An encounter might be a single cataclysmic event, such as repatriating to a passport country and discovering it feels strange and unfamiliar. As a global nomad friend of mine named Timothy put it, "We went back to

Canada, which I'd always thought of as home, but when we got there, I realized it was Mars."

Another adult global nomad, Hans, describes his experience: "I was really happy growing up in Germany, but I still had this thing in my mind that when I repatriated to the U.S. I'd be around Blacks and Hispanics, other biracial people like me. And then, when we did repatriate, I found out that I was different from the African-Americans and Latino Americans—I talked and walked and dressed differently. Those two groups especially ostracized me immediately."

A global nomad's encounter experience might also be an accumulation of events—like being asked for the tenth, twentieth, or fiftieth time "Where are you from?" and not being sure, yet again, how to answer.

Most global nomads have hundreds of potential encounter experiences by the time they reach adolescence, including childhood repatriations, before they have the one that actually wakes them up. For Timothy and Hans, sometimes repatriation is the spark that sets the search for identity congruence on fire. An adult global nomad named Leslie remembers that when she repatriated to a town of thirty thousand after having lived in capital cities all over the world and found "people so *local*, with no desire to go outside of town," she started questioning why and how she was so different.

In the past, it was not uncommon for a global nomad to move solidly into adulthood without having an encounter experience. In such cases, the encounter may grow out of a rising sense of dissatisfaction or even depression. A woman named Eliza, who had grown up in Kenya, told me: "I had a good relationship. I had a successful practice. I had all my ducks in a row, and yet I would wake up in the morning deeply depressed." Eventually, Eliza went into therapy. "My therapist knew nothing about global nomads... she just thought it was really neat that I'd grown up in all these different places. So she focused on the typical things, my relationship with my parents and my mother and blah, blah, blah, but one of the things that came up in discussion was that I was deciding to go to Kenya to live for a year. My therapist said, 'I don't understand why you're doing this. Give me the reasons.' And I started weeping and said, 'I just have to go.' It was like all my longing to be back with my roots. Kenya had become that other place. And I felt so much sadness... I started looking at that. I took that piece and I started saying, 'Well, this is interesting. Why is this so important to me?'"

Judith, a German global nomad, resisted a move with her husband to Singapore at first: "Moving from country to country wasn't what I wanted for my children. And so I moved to Singapore with a feeling of impending doom. But arriving there, I more or less instantaneously started to feel comfortable. The climate was very familiar to my time in Zimbabwe; the international and multicultural environment, too. So for the first time I started reading and reflecting on what it meant to have grown up globally. Before that, it was only a dim realization."

So how can you, as proactive parents, help your children with their encounter experiences? First of all, don't help them *avoid* encounter. Until they have an encounter experience, your kids won't be able to make sense of growing up globally, or ultimately to put all their skills, abilities, and deeply valuable knowledge to use. You don't want to rush your children into encounter, either, but they probably won't let you; adolescents are very good at ignoring sage parental advice until they're ready to find it useful. The point is to facilitate the process, whatever way their own particular life paths lead them to it.

Next, here's a provocative piece of information: in all my travels, conversations, and research, I've discovered that the only people who had relatively easy identity encounter experiences related to growing up globally were those who had been introduced to the terms "global nomad" and "third culture kid" while still living overseas, or those who were offered repatriation services upon coming "home" and heard the terms that way (or at least subset terms like "missionary kid," "oil brat," "military brat," and so on).

So here's a second key strategy for proactive parenting: introduce your children from their earliest years abroad to the terms "global nomad" and "third culture kid." They may not be interested at the time, but when they start searching for how to make meaning of their internationally mobile lives, they'll know there's this particularly relevant subject that people have written and spoken about.

3. Exploration

Once the sense of being different penetrates their defenses enough to make them wonder why, global nomads move developmentally into "exploration."

This process unfolds in two broad ways. If children already know the terms "global nomad" and "third culture kid," their experience of being different is contextualized. "Aha!" they exclaim. "Perhaps this has something to do with being a global nomad. Now, what was it Ms. Pascoe was talking about at that assembly?" And so they unfold the road map, allowing them, as time passes, to find the books to read, the websites to browse, the conferences to go to, the people to consult. They discover guideposts to show them the way forward.

Kids who don't know the terms, however, typically feel very much alone. Janet Bennett, executive director of the Intercultural Communication Institute, calls this feeling "terminal uniqueness." We know we feel different, but we don't know why, and we think we must be the only ones who've ever felt this way. Is there something wrong with us? Is that why don't we fit in? It doesn't usually occur to kids in this situation that the reason they're questioning themselves is because they grew up internationally. And, likewise, it doesn't occur to them to reach out to others who grew up internationally, too. They go forward guided only by their "gut feelings" and intuition. When you don't have a road map, the fact that you are different feels value-loaded with negative judgments, your own and those of your mainstream peers.

Ultimately, road map or none, a key task in global nomad identity development is the exploration of "national" identity: "What does it mean to me to be a citizen of this country on whose passport I travel?" "How do my worldview and values differ from or run parallel to those of my homegrown peers?"

Passports form an integral part of the global nomad's experience. Brandished at most border crossings, they proclaim nationality and citizenship. Nationality and citizenship also become defining characteristics of expatriate and repatriate communities.

International schools typically include as a measure of their "internationality" the number of nationalities represented among the student body. Annual "international days" encourage children to wear their national dress to school while you, the parent, prepare national cuisine for the food bazaar and speak about national customs in the classroom. When your children are new to a school, nationality is a defining parameter, in much the same way as the answer to the question "What does your father do?"

The concept of nationality presents global nomads with an interesting paradox. For many of us, nationality is relatively uninformative as a cultural descriptor, at least in the long term. While we're overseas, we're often quite content to accept our parents' assertion that we're British, or Mexican, or Moroccan. American global nomads can have the illusion reinforced even further by the prevalence of American popular culture around the world; you can think you know the U.S. well when you watch American television and eat at McDonald's. When we repatriate, however, that illusion is usually shattered. That's why repatriation is so typically an identity encounter experience, and that's why national identity is so typically a key ingredient in the global nomad's identity exploration.

My sister Marnie tells the story of coming home from high school in Houston, going up to my father's study and opening the file cabinet to find her passport, then looking at its assertion: "Nationality: United States of America." She would do this day after day, repeating to herself, as if it were a mantra, "I am American. I am American." We had just moved to Houston from Malaysia, our ninth international move, and it was a very difficult repatriation for all of us. Trying to figure out why she didn't fit in with the Houstonians around her, Marnie started to question her national identity.

Here's my third key strategy for proactively guiding your children: be careful, and intentional, about the ideas you foster in them about their national identity. Beware of setting up false expectations that they'll immediately feel "at home" when they repatriate. Your children's sense of nationality will probably be very different from your own.

Understandably, one of the ways parents often try to be proactive around this issue of national identity is to answer the question for their children. An expatriate parent from Zimbabwe told me how she once listened in horror as her four children answered in turn someone's innocent question "Where are you from?" with the name of the four different countries in which each of them had been born—none of them Zimbabwe. The parent said that, from then on, each time it came up she would correct them: "No, no, you're Zimbabwean." She didn't realize, however, that the illusion of belonging in Zimbabwe would probably break apart as soon as the children repatriated. The best way to minimize the upheaval of national identity questioning for your children is to broaden the territory from which an answer can be drawn. Don't make it a zero-sum game with only one right answer.

Here is my fourth key strategy for proactive parenting around issues of global nomad identity: accept, indeed advocate for the possibility, that your children can be both/and rather than either/or. In other words, let your children be Zimbabwean *and* British, Zimbabwean *and* Singaporean, Zimbabwean *and* Moroccan if that's what they want. Talk with them, as soon as you perceive them to be ready, about the possibility that rather than being "Zimbabwean," full stop, they may be "Zimbabwean global nomads"—Zimbabwean with an overlay of international interest, experience, expertise, and allegiance. This is perhaps a revolutionary idea in a time when nation-states are hardening their boundaries and borders, but I personally believe that it could be the saving of our world.

4. Integration

Identity exploration can go on for a few months or for many years, but at some point global nomads come to a place of congruence. We understand who we are in terms of our internationally mobile lives: how those lives have influenced us, shaped us, directed our interests and talents.

The transition from exploration to integration may be very gradual. One day something may remind us of our mobile childhoods, and we realize that we haven't talked about it recently or reflected lately on its influence on our lives. It's typically with this kind of hindsight that we understand we've completed the exploration our encounter experience sets in motion.

It's important to recognize that some people in integration may have high salience for having grown up globally, others not. That is, some of us may have explored our identity in light of our internationally mobile childhoods and found that it means a lot to us; others may complete exploration and discard the life history as irrelevant. Integration doesn't describe a single end point; it simply indicates that the life experience has been considered and congruence achieved.

People in integration are comfortable with being different from their homegrown peers. Janet Bennett of the Intercultural Communication Institute explains this when she writes about "cultural marginality" and "constructive marginals."

Cultural marginality, Bennett says, is the experience typical of people who have been moulded by exposure to two or more cultural traditions; they are on the cultural margins, rather than in the mainstream, of each of the cultures that influenced them. Constructive marginals are people who have considered why they're different and are comfortable with being so. Indeed, they're grateful for it; they use their difference to strengthen their competence and to maximize their personal and professional success. While they may not feel fully at home anywhere, constructively marginal global nomads feel somewhat at home *everywhere*—a very important distinction.

At the other end of the marginality continuum is the experience Bennett calls "encapsulated marginality." Encapsulated marginals are trapped by their feeling of being different; they never feel at home, have no clear sense of their values, and easily lose their sense of inner direction. Introducing your child at an early age to the terms "global nomad" and "third culture kid" will once again be helpful in easing their passage through repatriation encounters and explorations of national identity into a constructive experience of identity integration.

5. Recycling
Of course, we're not static as human beings. Identity development doesn't bring you to an end point but instead has the potential for continuing on in ever deepening

and expanding iterations. The identity literature calls this "identity recycling."

What the term means is that someday the global nomad will have another encounter experience to do with growing up globally. It probably won't be as intense as the first one, but it will be sufficiently "awakening" that once again she'll find herself reflecting on how her internationally mobile childhood has influenced her. She'll again engage in identity exploration, and again move through to identity integration.

Peter Adler, intercultural researcher and scholar, once described identity development as a process of "being in becoming." I love that phrase. It perfectly captures the identity development process of those who are most successful in today's complex world—people who stay open to learning and questioning and reflection as they continue through life.

Being a global nomad hasn't always been easy for me, and at times it's been downright painful. Yet it's one of the qualities of my life for which I am most grateful.

Would I value what I value today if I had not been raised globally? It's hard to say. But I do know that being a global nomad gave me the knowledge and skill I needed to develop competence. It's a mark of my own parents' good sense that they were able to guide me as well as they did even without a book such as Robin's to help them. I hope you're able to put the wisdom and sage advice in these pages into action. And as you do so, keep in mind my suggestions for guiding your children on this, their "most excellent journey" of identity development.

RESOURCES

BOOKS

Expatriate life

Bryson, Debra R., & Hoge, Charise M. 2006. *A Portable Identity: A Woman's Guide to Maintaining a Sense of Self while Moving Overseas.* Transition Press International.

Copeland, Anne. 2005. *Global Baby.* Interchange Institute.

Dehner, Haidee, & Dehner, Maya. 2001. *Life on the Outside: Memoirs of a Nomadic Mother and Daughter.* Wanderlust Press.

Eidse, Faith, & Sichel, Nina (Eds.). 2004. *Unrooted Childhoods: Memoirs of Growing Up Global.* Nicholas Brealey Publishing.

Hess, Melissa Brayer, & Linderman, Patricia. 2002. *The Expert Expatriate: Your Guide to Successful Relocation Abroad.* Nicholas Brealey Publishing.

Jehle-Caitcheon, Ngaire. 2003. *Parenting Abroad.* Aletheia Publications.

Kruempelman, Elizabeth. 2002. *The Global Citizen: A Guide to Creating an International Life and Career.* Ten Speed Press.

Malewski, Margaret. 2005. *GenXpat: The Young Professional's Guide to Making a Successful Life Abroad.* Intercultural Press.

Parfitt, Jo. 2002. *A Career in Your Suitcase 2.* Summertime Publishing.

Pascoe, Robin. 2000. *Homeward Bound: A Spouse's Guide to Repatriation.* Expatriate Press.

———. 2003. *A Moveable Marriage: Relocate Your Relationship without Breaking It.* Expatriate Press.

Pollock, David C., & Van Reken, Ruth E. 2001. *Third Culture Kids: The Experience of Growing Up among Worlds.* 2nd ed. Nicholas Brealey Publishing.

Romano, Dugan. 2001.
Intercultural Marriage: Promises and Pitfalls. 2nd ed. Nicholas Brealey Publishing.

Smith, Carolyn D. 1996.
Strangers at Home: Essays on the Effect of Living Overseas and Coming "Home" to a Strange Land. Aletheia Publications.

Van Reken, Ruth E. 1995. *Letters Never Sent: One Woman's Journey from Hurt to Wholeness.* Letters.

Parenting

Anderegg, David. 2003. *Worried All the Time: Overparenting in an Age of Anxiety and How to Stop It.* Free Press.

Hulbert, Ann. 2003. *Raising America: Experts, Parents, and a Century of Advice about Children.* Alfred A. Knopf.

Levine, Mel. 2002. *A Mind at a Time.* Simon & Schuster.

———. 2005. *Ready or Not, Here Life Comes.* Simon & Schuster.

Roberts, Anita. 2001. *Safe Teen: Powerful Alternatives to Violence.* Raincoast Books.

Stearns, Peter N. 2003. *Anxious Parents: A History of Modern Childrearing in America.* New York University Press.

Work-life balance

Friedman, Stewart D., & Greenhaus, Jeffrey H. 2000. *Work and Family: Allies or Enemies?* Oxford University Press.

Gordon, Gil. 2001. *Turn It Off: How to Unplug from the Anywhere-Anytime Office without Disconnecting Your Career.* Three Rivers Press.

Hendricks, William, & Coté, Jim. 1998. *On the Road Again: Travel, Love, and Marriage.* Fleming H. Revell.

Hochschild, Arlie Russell. 1997. *The Time Bind: When Work Becomes Home and Home Becomes Work.* Henry Holt & Co.

Hoekstra, Elizabeth M. 1998. *Keeping Your Family Close: When Frequent Travel Pulls You Apart.* Crossways Books.

Poelmans, Steven (Ed.). 2005. *Work and Family: An International Research Perspective.* Lawrence Erlbaum Associates.

Moving with children

Berenstain, Stan, & Berenstain, Jan. 1981. *The Berenstain Bears' Moving Day.* Random House for Young Readers.

Maxfield, Brenda. 2001. *Up, Up and Away! A Guide for Children and Their Parents Who Are Moving from One Culture to Another.* Foreign Service Youth Foundation.

Miller, Susan. 1995. *After the Boxes Are Unpacked: Moving On after Moving In.* Tyndale House Publishers.

Roman, Beverly. *Home Away from Home: Turning Your International Relocation into a Lifetime Enhancement.* BR Anchor Books.

Schubeck, Carol M. 2000. *Let's Move Together.* SuitCase Press.

USEFUL WEBSITES

Celebrate the TCK Journey
http://celebratethetckjourney.com
From author and educator Haidee Dehner, who wrote *Life on the Outside* with her daughter Maya. Check out the TCK activity kit CD, which advisors and teachers who piloted this unit praise for its effectiveness with third culture kids.

All Kinds of Minds
www.allkindsofminds.org
This fantastic parenting resource site is that of Dr. Mel Levine, whose books are quoted in this book.

Family Life Abroad
www.familylifeabroad.com
Numerous articles make up this website, which lives up to its name. Contributions are from a wide variety of sources.

Foreign Service Youth Foundation
www.fsyf.org
This organization provides information, outreach, and support for the internationally mobile families of U.S. Foreign Affairs agencies.

Interaction International
www.tckinteract.net
The world's foremost organization advocating on behalf of third culture kids of all ages, nations, and backgrounds. Interaction International has been spanning the globe, working tirelessly to make the lives of every TCK and their families count.

Travel with Your Kids
www.travelwithyourkids.com
This is a great site for families living abroad that combines fun things to do with practical information for planning trips.

Families in Global Transition
www.figt.org
The website of the Families in Global Transition conference provides strategic resources for families and individuals who live, move, and work throughout the world.

Transition Dynamics
www.transition-dynamics.com
This is the website of interculturalist Barbara Schaetti. It features many useful articles as well as writings from children themselves. Parents will find it very helpful.

International Schools Services
www.iss.edu
A nonprofit corporation dedicated to excellence for children attending overseas schools worldwide, ISS is the world's leader in providing a comprehensive range of quality educational services for schools, educators, families, and corporations.

American Psychological Association
www.apa.org/international
The international section of this American association can offer resources for parents seeking counseling abroad.

American Association for Marriage and Family Therapy
www.aamft.org
Parents seeking professional help should check out this site.

The Trailing Spouse
www.thetrailingspouse.com
The website of Yvonne McNulty, an academic and expat spouse and mother researching spousal and expatriate issues. It contains many articles and current research on expatriation.

Career in Your Suitcase
www.career-in-your-suitcase
The website of author Joanna Parfitt, which can help expat spouses find satisfying work while living abroad.

ABOUT THE AUTHOR

 **ROBIN PASCOE** is well known to traveling spouses internationally for her humorous, compassionate, and encouraging presentations to expatriate communities, human resource groups, and corporate gatherings around the world. As well as writing countless articles and making many media appearances, Robin has written four previous books on the subject of global living and adjustment. Her personal experiences of packing and unpacking her life, marriage, and family throughout Asia were the inspiration for exploring the challenges and joys inherent to the expatriate lifestyle. Her popular website, Expat Expert.com, is a treasure trove of information, opinion, and humour for expatriate families. Robin currently lives in North Vancouver, Canada.

ABOUT THE CONTRIBUTORS

BARBARA F. SCHAETTI, PHD, is founder and principal of Transition Dynamics and one of the three founding partners of Personal Leadership Seminars LLC. A dual national (American and Swiss), Schaetti grew up in ten countries on five continents. With experience since 1985 in both the private and public sectors, she has a particular passion for helping people cultivate their core intercultural capacity. She has served on the board of directors of Families in Global Transition.

LOIS J. BUSHONG, MS, LMFT, grew up in Latin America, where her parents served as missionaries. She works as a licensed marriage and family therapist at Eagle Creek Counseling in Indianapolis, Indiana, where her clientele includes internationals in transition, missionaries, expatriates, repatriates, and adult third culture kids. She serves as adjunct faculty with Indiana Wesleyan University in the Graduate Counseling Department and is also on the board of directors of Families in Global Transition.

PRAISE FOR ROBIN'S PREVIOUS BOOKS AND WEBSITE

"*A Moveable Marriage* is a masterpiece! You so candidly explain the feelings and realities of the family and spouse in a relocation."
~ CHERYL RANASINGHE, KOREA

"I have finally finished reading *Homeward Bound*. It took me three months but I am so glad that I read it!"
~ GABBI LEININGER

"I could have listened to you for hours as you make people feel connected, Robin. We were all very moved by your talk and the subjects of your books."
~ JOAN BROWN, GERMANY

"I just wanted to thank you for creating a website of your experiences and for making me laugh, Robin!! I was amazed at how uncanny your stories were of meeting other expat wives."
~ RACHAEL NEVILE, BAHRAIN

CPSIA information can be obtained at www.ICGtesting.com
Printed in the USA
BVOW03s2322080416

443173BV00001B/11/P